Rank and Warfare among the Plains Indians

BERNARD MISHKIN

RANK AND WARFARE
AMONG THE PLAINS INDIANS

Introduction to the Bison Book Edition
by Morris W. Foster

University of Nebraska Press
Lincoln and London

Copyright 1940 by Bernard Mishkin
Introduction to the Bison Book Edition copyright © 1992 by
the University of Nebraska Press
All rights reserved
Manufactured in the United States of America

First Bison Book printing: 1992
Most recent printing indicated by the last digit below:
10   9   8   7   6   5   4   3   2   1

Library of Congress Cataloging-in-Publication Data
Mishkin, Bernard, 1913–
Rank and warfare among the Plains Indians / Bernard Mishkin; introduction to the
Bison Book edition by Morris W. Foster.
p.   cm.
Originally published: Seattle: University of Washington Press, 1940. (Monographs
of the American Ethnological Society; 3)
ISBN 0-8032-8185-4
1. Kiowa Indians—Wars.   2. Kiowa Indians—Social conditions.   3. Kiowa Indians—History.   I. Title.
e99.K5M57   1992
978'.004974—dc20
92-15035   CIP

Reprinted by arrangement with the University of Washington Press. Originally
published in 1940 as Monograph 3 of the American Ethnological Society.

INTRODUCTION
by Morris W. Foster

The North American Plains became widely known to Anglo-Americans through popular accounts of its exploration and colonization in the nineteenth century. Through these images, prominently marketed in dime novels and wild West shows, Plains Indians entered into American mythology as fierce nomadic warriors who cared more about personal honor than about the outcome of any larger conflict (Ewers 1965). This portrayal, which has become the standard representation of Plains peoples in the twentieth century, has endured because it is consistent with the idea of nobility in defeat. By referring to the Plains Indian as a competitor who insisted on fighting in such a way that it was inevitable he should lose, Anglo-Americans have justified their usurpation of the Great Plains.

For the most part, the first half-century of Anglo scholarship about the Plains peoples replicated this theme, though somewhat less colorfully than in the popular media. Anthropologists such as Clark Wissler (1914, 1922) and historians such as George Grinnell (1923) and Rupert Richardson (1933) accepted the notion of a fierce, highly individualistic militarism as the basis for nomadic Plains social organization. Even for anthropologists Robert Lowie (1927, 1954) and E. Adamson Hoebel (1940, 1954), more sophisticated social theorists, a psychological propensity for violence was a sufficient explanation for features of Plains social organization.

Thus, as a result both of popular and academic imagery, Plains peoples have become closely identified with nomadic military activities, especially hostile encounters with Euro-Americans. However, while those encounters certainly occurred, they were not necessarily the defining moments for the native communities involved. And while warfare was a significant aspect of everyday community life, it was not necessarily more significant to the arrangement of social organization than is warfare in contemporary Anglo-American society. In 1780, Comanches went to war with the Spanish over access to New Mexican markets. In 1991, the United States went to war with Iraq over access to Kuwaiti oil. Although we might, in both examples, debate the definition of "war," that debate will not diminish the underlying economic motivations at work in each. Plains scholars have, for the most part, been as reluctant as Anglo politicians to treat explicitly the economic bases for warfare. This reluctance derives, in part, from the idealization of the Great Plains in the academic literature.

Most anthropologists who studied American Indian peoples prior to World War II were uninterested in the contemporaneous reservation and post-allotment communities they visited. Instead, they wanted to get at what were to them the more "pristine" ways of life of the pre-reservation era. Thus, those anthropologists worked primarily with elderly informants who might recall a time when their communities were not confined to reservations or allotments or who had heard the stories of elders who had lived in those days. The descriptive studies based on these memories often used the rhetorical device of the ethnographic present in which the pre-reservation communities were described as if they still existed.

By telescoping time, anthropologists and their informants were engaged in a sort of mythologizing in which the past became the timeless present. The pre-reservation era became an ideal that was not part of historical time. Only by assuming that the pre-reservation period was relatively immune from external historical forces and was more or less unchanging from contact through the late nineteenth century could anthropologists represent their informants' information as ethnography. By denying history in order to maintain the validity of the ethnographic present, anthropologists also denied themselves the means to distinguish pre-contact from post-contact eras.

A good example of this logic is the traditional anthropological interpretation of the role of the horse on the post-contact Plains. That interpretation argued that the horse did not qualitatively change the pattern of Plains sociocultural organization as established in the prehistoric period. Instead, the horse was portrayed as incrementally contributing to already developed prehistoric patterns (e.g., Lowie 1954). The incrementalist interpretation validated the practice of projecting what was known of late-nineteenth-century and early-twentieth-century Plains communities back in time to reconstruct pre-reservation ways of life. Once it is admitted that an external factor like the horse could have transformed Plains communities, that they were in fact subject to historical time, then any retrospective reconstruction is open to question.

Another conceptual device that insulated our images of native communities from historical and other external conditions was the anthropological concept of the tribe. Most anthropological studies began and ended with the tribal unit, as if external relations with others were of little consequence for internal social and cultural organization. This, of course, was a further idealization of native peoples that contributed to their representation as historically timeless communities. By ignoring the consequences of changing external relations, except for the occasional borrowing of material and religious features, anthropologists could discount the significance of history in their interpretations of internal sociocultural arrangements.

Tribes were described as though they were detached, static features of the physical landscape of the Great Plains and not interrelated dynamic features of its changing social landscape. In this view, tribes were buffeted by but not implicated in the events that surrounded them until the "end"—that is, the institution of reservations. Indeed, with the coming of reservations in the late nineteenth century, anthropologists often portrayed native peoples as though they were survivors stumbling out of some time capsule into a world beyond previous experience (e.g., Wallace and Hoebel 1952).

Curiously as this tradition of ahistorical, tribe-specific scholarship flourished, a tradition of explicating each part of the Plains culture area in reference to the whole also was established. The practice of dividing native North America into regional culture areas was established as a means for organizing exhibits at the Pan-American Exposition of 1893 and spread from there to museums and academic scholarship (Mason 1896; Holmes 1903). The theory of culture areas was codified by Wissler (1926) and Kroeber (1939) on the basis of environmental constraints that narrowly delimited the range of social and cultural features native peoples successfully could employ. Thus, what began as a practice for conveniently displaying material artifacts became, over time, a practice of geographically stereotyping sociocultural entities.

Like the concept of the tribe, the concept of the culture area also ignored history and intercommunity relations by its treatment of internal social and cultural organization. By emphasizing similarities, it enabled scholars to speak of a singular Plains culture or society. In effect, this practice treated the entire culture area as one tribe. The concept of a single Plains sociocultural unit made it unnecessary to take account of the constantly changing territorial relations among Plains peoples during the historic period, changes that reflected differing political and economic relations both among native communities and between those communities and Euro-Americans. The culture area, tied to enduring features of the physical landscape rather than to more ephemeral features of the sociocultural landscape, was, like the concepts of the ethnographic present and the tribe, a further means for constructing a mythic, timeless image of the Plains.

In this context, Bernard Mishkin's study of the economic bases for Plains Indian warfare and rank was iconoclastic. Mishkin outlined an argument that, for the first time, linked the individual pursuit of social status through military activities to the communal economics of Plains life. The key to this linkage was the horse. In contrast to traditional ideas of the Plains, Mishkin (p. 8) asserted that the advent of the horse transformed native social organizations and cultural values: "The role the horse played in the economic life of the Plains people and the extent to which it influenced their culture cannot be exaggerated" (p. 8). The horse, according to Mishkin's thesis, served both as a means and as an end in the post-contact transformation of Plains communities.

The horse increased mobility on the Plains and made greater intercommunity interaction possible. As Mishkin interpreted it, greater mobility not only facilitated trade among communities, it also made warfare between them a more frequent occurrence. This increasing interaction contributed to the formation of a more homogeneous Plains culture area, both by opportunities for peaceable intercommunity communication and, in hostilities, through a uniform requirement for military behavior. In Mishkin's view, the conditions of the military horse race on the Plains were just as formative as the economic opportunities that the horse market afforded native communities.

Mishkin portrayed Plains warfare as essentially an individual enterprise. Among the Kiowas, with whom Mishkin conducted oral historical fieldwork in 1935, raiding and revenge parties were organized without the sanction of any larger social unit. While the actions of raiding party members generally were coordinated, individual acts of bravery in battle were valued over actions that could not be attributed to the initiative of a single participant. It was individual acts that were recounted later as claims for the social advancement of Kiowa warriors in community gatherings.

Thus, an important by-product of warfare, aside from communal territorial and economic outcomes, was the individual achievement of social status. This made the communal accommodation and regulation of individual status or rank gained through warfare a central problem in the post-contact realignment of Plains social organizations. How could competition among warriors and the more ephemeral social units they led (raiding and revenge parties, local bands, and age cohorts) be regulated so that the larger community and its more permanent constituent units (named divisions, military societies, and religious organizations) maintained order and solidarity? Without some means for subjecting the individual enterprise of warfare to communal regulation, the enduring features of community social structure would have fragmented into self-interested economic and political pieces.

As Mishkin notes for the Kiowa, an elaborate system of etiquette developed around military activities and their subsequent recounting. An important function of this system was to subject individual warriors to communal regulation. Although warriors were granted status through their military actions, those actions were circumscribed by notions of appropriate behavior. Among the most highly valued military acts were covering the retreat of a war party by charging the enemy and rescuing a comrade. Such valuations channeled individual behavior toward the good of the war party as a group and, as Mishkin also observed, often forced warriors to choose between acquiring status or acquiring horses. The requirement that military deeds such as these be legitimized in public narrations gave the larger community the opportunity to evaluate claims to higher rank, screening individual warriors who were attempting to use military acts to achieve leadership positions. Because consistently conspicuous generosity was expected of those with high rank, individuals who pursued status were bound still further to community regulation. Thus, while high rank was a token of economic success, it also had its economic costs and may even be thought of as a means for constraining the accumulation of both status and wealth.

As Mishkin pointed out, individuals who achieved status in warfare almost always acquired horses at the same time. This entanglement of status and wealth through individual action also created problems for Plains social organizations. Differentials of wealth among individuals, families, and extra-familial social units posed similar difficulties for social order and solidarity as did the individual achievement of social status. In addition, the increased flow of economic goods such as horses through native communities required new conventions for regulating their distribution, valuation, and exchange in respect both to other tangible goods and to intangible social worth.

The horse was, arguably, as ubiquitously useful in the post-contact world of the Plains as was the bison in the prehistoric Plains. Horses not only provided transportation, they also were measures of individual wealth and generosity within communities, were in heavy demand as trade items in both Indian and Euro-American markets, and may have served as a significant food source (an idea largely overlooked by most scholars of the Plains). Most of the horses on the pre-reservation Plains were acquired through raiding, thus their status as economic goods accelerated the warfare. The traditional view has been that Plains communities were primarily end users of horses captured in raids (Lowie 1954). However, we are only just now beginning to understand the extent to which external markets driven both by Euro-American and indigenous demand affected the organization of Plains communities like those of the Kiowa and Comanche that specialized in the emerging horse trade (Foster 1991).

Although the Kiowa made use of leveling mechanisms, as noted above, to redistribute some of the wealth accumulated through raiding and trading activities, theirs was not an egalitarian society. Instead, the advantages of wealth were passed on from one generation to another through what Mishkin called a caste system of inherited rank. More precisely, a man inherited the economic advantage or disadvantage of his family's rank. Those born into families of high rank were not under the pressure of everyday life to acquire horses and other goods through raiding and so could afford to engage in military activities primarily in pursuit of rank. Conversely, a man whose family lacked economic means was, in the first place, dependent upon others for mounts to engage in military activities (and to whom he subsequently owed a share of his spoils), was motivated to behave in ways that maximized the number of horses he acquired in a raid rather than engage in status-achieving acts, and may have found the generosity required of high rank to be economically onerous in any event. Kiowa social stratification in combination with the public etiquette of rank resulted in a careful balancing of the economic and social productivity of warfare in a manner that maintained the Kiowa community while adapting to the larger political economy beyond its boundaries.

Mishkin's interpretation of Kiowa society remains an important source alongside the previous work of Mooney (1898), the contemporaneous work of Richardson (1940), and the subsequent work of Marriot (1945, 1968) and Levy (1959). Because of the richness of information in both published and unpublished treatments of the Kiowa, a historical reinterpretation of their community is overdue. The insights provided by Mishkin and the others are limited by their partial understandings of the historical development and context of the Plains. Even Mishkin occasionally reverts to the traditional anthropological imagery of warlike Plains Indians and the device of the ethnographic present. A full articulation of the ethnological and historical dimensions of Kiowa social life promises a surprising revision of the traditional interpretation of the Kiowa community.

Mishkin's work is now more than fifty years old and has become an obligatory citation in subsequent studies of the Plains. But, many of Mishkin's insights have been neglected. Mishkin's views were part of an alternative movement in Plains scholarship that briefly flowered in the period just before and after World War II but which, for various reasons, did not reproduce itself in the next generation of Plains scholars. While some of the ideas of the alternative movement were incorporated into the more established tradition of Plains scholarship, the model that these works established was not widely replicated.

Along with Esther Goldfrank (1945), Preston Holder (1970), Joseph Jablow (1950), Alexander Lesser (1933), Oscar Lewis (1942), Jane Richardson (1940), Frank Secoy (1953), and Gene Weltfish (1965), Mishkin presented a challenge to prevailing ideas of the Plains based on the detailed ethnographic or historical study of one or more native communities. Their studies took a more dynamic, heterogeneous view of Plains communities. They emphasized discontinuities with the prehistoric past, and highlighted increasing involvement in the emerging Euro-American political economy and the consequent necessity of adapting intracommunity social organizations to those changed circumstances. Significantly, each of these scholars was trained at Columbia University, Lesser and Weltfish under Franz Boas and the others under the post-Boasian influence of Ruth Benedict and W. Duncan Strong. The direction in which this group of scholars was headed belies the traditional view of Boas and his immediate successors at Columbia as ahistorical, particularistic, and theoretically unsophisticated.

Despite this alternative movement, though, the mainstream of Plains scholarship remained in the tradition of Robert Lowie and Clark Wissler, stewarded and occasionally revitalized by such scholars as Fred Eggan (1966), E. Adamson Hoebel (1954), Symmes Oliver (1962), Frank Roe (1955), and Clyde Wilson (1963). While their specific studies of Plains communities are by no means inferior, these works cumulatively present a different view of Plains peoples: as more homogeneous, less affected by Euro-American contact, and with social organizations determined more by the Plains environment than by external economic conditions.

The traditional emphasis on the Plains environment, revitalized as cultural ecology in the 1960s, pushed aside the alternative cohort's emphasis on the political economy of the Plains, to become the basis for much of Plains scholarship in the post–World War II period. One reason for this has been the decline in ethnological interest in the Plains, and in American Indian communities in general, at the same time as archaeological interest has increased. Archaeologists have found environmental and ecological analogies from historic to prehistoric times compelling. The largely economic arguments of scholars such as Mishkin do not support using historical analogies for prehistoric explanation.

There also were institutional reasons for the competitive failure of the alternative movement. Of the scholars who were part of it, only Lesser, Weltfish, Goldfrank, and Holder made their careers as active Plains researchers. Perhaps most significantly, though, none of this cohort held an academic position in a major graduate department of anthropology for any extended period of time, thus limiting their influence among future generations of anthropologists. In contrast, the successors to Wissler and Lowie listed above were active in Plains research over most of their careers, were tenured in major graduate departments where subsequent generations of Plains scholars were trained, reviewed article and book manuscripts for publication, and were looked to as authorities on the Plains by anthropologists and historians who lacked a Plains specialization. Lack of power in the discipline, lack of students, lack of a major university's prestige all contributed to the muted influence of the alternative movement in Plains scholarship.

Bernard Mishkin's career is a good example of the institutional problems his ideas have encountered (Wagley 1955). He received his Ph.D. from Columbia in 1937 at the age of twenty-four for his study of Plains rank and warfare. By the time Mishkin's monograph was published in 1940, he had already gone on to fieldwork in New Guinea and highland Peru. After service in World War II, he held several post-doctoral positions in connection with his interest in South America and taught for two academic years at Brandeis. He eventually left academics to become an airline executive, and died in 1954. The Plains monograph was Mishkin's only publication on a Plains topic.

Despite his brief engagement with the Plains, Mishkin's ideas are once again at issue in Plains scholarship. Building on the work of John Ewers (1955, 1968), who continued to pursue economic topics while all about him were focused on ecological topics, scholars such as Patricia Albers and William James (1986, 1991), Donald Blakeslee (1975), Alan Klein (1977, 1980), Susan Vehik (1988), and W. Raymond Wood (1972, 1973, 1980) have contributed to a more detailed elucidation of pre- and post-contact Plains trade networks. Although a synthetic treatment has yet to be published, these studies suggest that a regional political economy based on trading indigenous and Euro-American goods may have been more significant in the post-contact period than were individual subsistence economies based on horticulture and bison hunting. Histories of specific Plains peoples that attend closely to the consequences of that external political economy for changes in intra-community social organization are now beginning to appear. (Fowler 1982, 1987; Foster 1991).

As studies of Plains communities become more historical, the importance of a regional political economy becomes primary and the explanatory power of traditional models that emphasize environment and ecology is lessened. The ecological limitations of the Plains environment remain useful in scholarly explanations as constraints on the activities and social units of native communities, but are less successful as motivations for communal behavior and organization. At least in academic discourse, images of the Plains are being transformed from those of a unique geographic place to ones of dynamic social interaction, both peaceable and violent. As Mishkin demonstrates in the following study, hostile interactions are explicable through an understanding of the peaceable relations that existed both within and without Plains communities. Far from being fierce individualists, the mythic counterparts of Anglo cowboys, Plains warriors were the focus for much of the articulation between the moral communities of which they were members and the political economy that defined the Plains in historic times. Warfare and trade were external manifestations of that nexus and rank was one means for internally rationalizing the social consequences of those undertakings.

Bibliography

Albers, Patricia and William James. Historical Materialism vs. Evolutionary Ecology: A Methodological Note on Horse Distribution and American Plains Indians. *Critique of Anthropology* 6(1):87–100, 1986.

———. Horses without People: A Critique of Neoclassical Ecology. In *Explorations in Political Economy: Essays in Criticism*, edited by R. K. Kanth and E. K. Hunt. Savage, Md.: Rowman and Littlefield Publishers, Inc., 1991.

Blakeslee, Donald J. The Plains Interband Trade System: An Ethnohistoric and Archaeological Investigation. Ph.D. dissertation. University of Wisconsin–Milwaukee. Ann Arbor: University Microfilms, 1975.

Eggan, Fred. *The American Indian: Perspectives for the Study of Social Change*. Chicago: Aldine, 1966.

Ewers, John C. *The Horse in Blackfoot Indian Culture*. Bureau of American Ethnology, Bulletin 159. Washington, D.C.: Government Printing Office, 1955.

———. The Emergence of the Plains Indian as the Symbol of the North American Indian. *Smithsonian Institution Annual Report for 1964*. Washington, D.C.: Government Printing Office, 1965.

———. *Indian Life on the Upper Missouri*. Norman: University of Oklahoma Press, 1968.

Foster, Morris W. *Being Comanche: A Social History of an American Indian Community*. Tucson: University of Arizona Press, 1991.

Fowler, Loretta. *Arapahoe Politics, 1851–1978: Symbols in Crises of Authority*. Lincoln: University of Nebraska Press, 1982.

———. *Shared Symbols, Contested Meanings: Gros Ventre Culture and History, 1778–1984*. Ithaca, N.Y.: Cornell University Press, 1987.

Goldfrank, Esther. *Changing Configurations in the Social Organization of a Blackfoot Tribe during the Reserve Period*. American Ethnological Society Monograph 8, 1945.

Grinnell, George B. *The Cheyenne Indians*. 2 volumes. New Haven: Yale University Press, 1923.

Hoebel, E. Adamson. *The Political Organization and Law-ways of the Comanche Indians*. American Anthropological Society Memoir 54, 1940.

———. *The Law of Primitive Man: A Study in Comparative Legal Dynamics*. Cambridge: Harvard University Press, 1954.

Holder, Preston. *The Hoe and the Horse on the Plains*. Lincoln: University of Nebraska Press, 1970.

Holmes, W. H. Classification and Arrangement of the Exhibits of an Anthropological Museum. *Annual Report of the Smithsonian Institution for 1901*, 1903.

Jablow, Joseph. *The Cheyenne in Plains Indian Trade Relations 1795–1840*. American Ethnological Society Monograph 12, 1950.

Klein, Alan M. Adaptive Strategies and Process on the Plains: The Nineteenth Century Cultural Sink. Ph.D. dissertation. State University of New York at Buffalo. Ann Arbor: University Microfilms, 1977.

————. Plains Economic Analysis: The Marxist Complement. In *Anthropology on the Great Plains*, edited by W. Raymond Wood and Margot Liberty. Lincoln: University of Nebraska Press, 1980.

Kroeber, Alfred L. *Cultural and Natural Areas of Native North America*. University of California Publications in American Archaeology and Ethnology 38, 1939.

Lesser, Alexander. The Pawnee Ghost Dance Hand Game. *Columbia University Contributions to Anthropology* 16:1–337, 1933.

Levy, Jerrold. *After Custer: Kiowa Political and Social Organization from the Reservation Period to the Present*. Ph.D. dissertation. University of Chicago, 1959.

Lewis, Oscar. *The Effects of White Contact on Blackfoot Culture*. American Ethnological Society Monograph 6, 1942.

Lowie, Robert. *Origin of the State*. New York: Harcourt Brace, 1927.

————. *Indians of the Plains*. New York: American Museum of Natural History, 1954.

Marriot, Alice. *The Ten Grandmothers*. Norman: University of Oklahoma Press, 1945.

————. *Kiowa Years: A Study in Cultural Impact*. New York: Macmillan and Co., 1968.

Mason, O. T. Influence of Environment upon Human Industries or Arts. *Annual Report of the Smithsonian Institution for 1895*. Washington, D.C.: Government Printing Office, 1896.

Mooney, James. Calendar History of the Kiowa Indians. *Bureau of American Ethnology Seventeenth Annual Report*. Washington, D.C.: Government Printing Office, 1898.

Oliver, Symmes C. Ecology and Cultural Continuity as Contributing Factors in the Social Organization of Plains Indians. *University of California Publications in American Archaeology and Ethnology* 43:1–90.

Richardson, Jane. *Law and Status among the Kiowa Indians*. American Ethnological Society Monograph 1, 1940.

Richardson, Rupert. *The Comanche Barrier to Southern Plains Settlement*. Glendale, Ca: Arthur H. Clark Co., 1933.

Roe, Frank G. *The Indian and the Horse*. Norman: University of Oklahoma Press, 1955.

Secoy, Frank R. *Changing Military Patterns on the Great Plains*. American Ethnological Society Monograph 21, 1953.

Vehik, Susan C. Late Prehistoric Exchange on the Southern Plains and its Periphery. *Midcontinental Journal of Archaeology* 13(1):41–68.

Wagley, Charles. Bernard Mishkin, 1913–1954. *American Anthropologist* 57:1033–35, 1955.

Wallace, Ernest and E. Adamson Hoebel. *The Comanches: Lords of the Southern Plains*. Norman: University of Oklahoma Press, 1952.

Weltfish, Gene. *The Lost Universe: The Way of Life of the Pawnees*. New York: Basic Books, 1965.

Wilson, Clyde. An Inquiry into the Nature of Plains Indian Cultural Development. *American Anthropologist* 65:335–69, 1963.

Wissler, Clark. The Influence of the Horse in the Development of Plains Culture. *American Anthropologist* 16:1–25, 1914.

———. *North American Indians of the Plains*. New York: American Museum of Natural History, 1922.

———. *The Relation of Man to Nature in Aboriginal North America*. New York: D. Appleton-Century Co., 1926.

Wood, W. Raymond. Contrastive Features of Native North American Trade Systems. In *For the Chief: Essays in Honor of Luther S. Cressman*, edited by F. Voget and R. Stephenson. University of Oregon Anthropological Papers 4, 1972.

———. Northern Plains Village Cultures: Internal Stability and External Relationships. *Journal of Anthropological Research* 30:1–16, 1973.

———. Plains Trade in Prehistoric and Protohistoric Intertribal Relations. In *Anthropology on the Great Plains*, edited by W. R. Wood and M. Liberty. Lincoln: University of Nebraska Press, 1980.

PREFACE

The Kiowa data in this study were collected among the Kiowa Indians of Oklahoma during the summer of 1935 under the auspices of the Laboratory of Anthropology of Santa Fé. The field party was directed by Dr. Alexander Lesser of Columbia University to whom I am indebted both for guidance in the field and for assistance in the preparation of the manuscript. To the other members of the field party, William Bascom, Donald Collier, R. Weston LaBarre, and Jane Richardson, I am indebted for their sum contribution for this study—for the field work was a cooperative venture. I thank them for agreeing that I might draw upon the pooled results of the field work in treating the problem I present here.

For criticism of, and assistance in the preparation of the manuscript I am deeply obligated to Professor Ruth Benedict. I am also obligated to Dr. Gene Weltfish for the use of her Pawnee field notes.

TABLE OF CONTENTS

		Page
I.	Introduction: The Problem	1
II.	The Horse in Plains Culture	5
III.	Outlines of Kiowa Society	24
IV.	Kiowa Warfare	28
V.	Kiowa Rank	35
	Appendix to Rank	54
VI.	Rank and Warfare in the Plains: Conclusions	57
VII.	Works Cited	64

I. Introduction: The Problem

The Indians of the North American Plains are familiar to laymen and students alike as the horse-riding, buffalo-hunting peoples of the west. The outlines of culture in the whole area are well-known, and the type features of Plains economic, social and religious life, have been frequently described.[1] The area included settled agriculturists as well as nomadic hunters, but many features of culture were common to both types of economic adjustment. Outstanding among the type features of Plains life is the characteristic pattern of warfare, in the form of raids and revenge parties, and the ways in which men achieved status and renown in terms of their war exploits.

Throughout most of the year, companies of warriors usually numbering from five to thirty men went off against their enemy. Membership in a war party was voluntary[2] and leadership went to the man who took the initiative and enlisted a number of warriors or obtained supernatural authorization. Most war parties consisted of a handful of men, but occasionally in some tribes, of as many as several hundred, even perhaps all the fighting men of the tribe.[3]

The usual war party of a few quick moving men was well suited

---

[1] See for example, the general description in C. Wissler, *Indians of the Plains*; and for specific peoples the monographs of——Denig, J. O. Dorsey, Fletcher and La Flesche, Grinnell, Kroeber, Lowie, Skinner, Wissler and others.

[2] It is difficult to know how far the voluntary character of Plains warfare went. There is good reason to believe that all men but the physically disabled at one time or another joined the parties. It is also patent that some men were more successful than others which would give rise to relative specialization of this class in war. Whether there was a tacit understanding of the minimum number of war parties the common man should attend is conceivable but not explicit. Moreover pressure was certainly put upon unwilling heroes. Membership in a men's society might sometimes influence the degree of participation in military life.

[3] Among the Crow, Blackfoot, Assiniboine, Comanche and Kiowa one to three men sometimes constituted the force. See M. Smith—*The War Complex of the Plains Indians*, Am. Philosophy Soc. Proc., V. 77. On the other hand, 200 to 300 warriors would leave the Kiowa tribal camp after the Sun Dance and pitched battles were known in some parts of the Plains. See Matthew, *Ethnography and Philology of the Hidatsa Indians* (U. S. Geological Survey, Haydn Misc. Publications, v. 7, 1877, p. 61).

to the form of warfare preferred on the Plains, the surprise attack. War parties fell upon the enemy unannounced. Such surprise attacks, conducted on the principle of quick withdrawal, did not permit concerted defense, and hence warfare was mainly of the aggressive type. One side attacked stealthily and the other side was more or less compelled to suffer the attack and to retaliate later, if possible, when the victors were themselves unprepared and unsuspecting. Defensive warfare, however, was sometimes practiced, chiefly among the village peoples. The Omaha, for example, had a highly developed system of defensive war which demanded ceremonial rites distinct from those of an aggressive war party. In the defensive tactics breast works might be thrown up by the women so that if the men were hard pressed they could retire to them. These defensive tactics might also be used outside of permanent villages, for instance on the seasonal hunt when they encountered a hostile tribe.

But even in the relatively rare defensive combat, actual forms of fighting were the same as in the typical aggressive warfare. Plains warfare had in fact little formally conducted combat: there was no division of function in fighting among different kinds of troops; there was no special kind of charging array;[4] and though all were under the orders of the leader each man fought independently selecting an enemy and disposing of him as best he could.

Each man's display of courage in combat and the performance of certain deeds were highly esteemed and added to his prestige. The counting of coup (touching an enemy with the hand or with a weapon, usually formalized in the Plains to counting coup on an enemy corpse), the taking of a scalp, a horse, gun and the killing of an enemy were honorific accomplishments. Individual warriors strained to become the recipients of these honors. Those who were successful constituted the elite in the community. In Plains society social position hinged mainly on achievement in war.

Although the male population of a Plains tribe could be divided into two broad classes—the warriors who had arrived and those who had not, distinctions were also made within the ranking

---

[4] Plains warriors, when the choice was given them, preferred to fight on foot. For example, see MOONEY, *Calendar History of the Kiowa*, 17th Annual Report of the Bureau of American Ethnology, 1895–96, Part I, p. 291.

group. Some valorous deeds were more highly regarded than others and an individual took his place in the rank hierarchy according to his particular war record. The method of "scoring" war records in one tribe did not differ materially from that operative in another. All the methods uniformly allowed for gradations in a more or less schematic way. So, among the Crow there were four deeds roughly graded on the basis of the honor they brought: counting coup, tearing a bow or gun out of the hands of the enemy, stealing a picketed horse from the midst of a hostile village and acting in the capacity of leader of the war party.[5]

The Ponca, in the eastern Plains, had a stricter grading of honorific deeds. Counting coup on an unwounded enemy was the deed of greatest bravery. Next came, in order of status-giving, counting coup on a fallen enemy, counting second coup,[6] killing an enemy, taking a scalp and capturing horses from an enemy.[7]

The exaggerated interest of warriors in the performance of war deeds in order to acquire rank and the standardized character of these deeds have led some interpreters of Plains culture to see warfare as a game in which the players maneuver for social recognition.[8] According to this widely accepted view, the pattern of Plains warfare is an elaborately developed activity separated from the normal current of Plains life and in which ambitious men engage to dissipate their over-aggressiveness, cut their capers, and win the laurels accompanying game-like performances in battle.

In stressing the individual psychological elements in warfare, students of Plains culture have not totally neglected to note the presence of an economic factor.[9] Indeed the motive of economic gain in military adventure is obvious enough in the description of any Plains tribe.[10] However the true weight and implications of

---

[5] LOWIE, *The Crow Indians*, p. 216.

[6] Many of the eastern Plains tribes count two coups, the second carrying less honor than the first. In other places in the Plains coup is counted one, three or four times, the first having greater value than those that follow, M. SMITH, *The War Complex of the Plains Indians*.

[7] FLETCHER and LA FLESCHE, *The Omaha Tribe*, RBAE, 27th, 1905–06, pp. 439–440.

[8] LOWIE, *Primitive Society*, p. 356.

[9] For example, GRINNELL, *Cheyenne Indians*, V. 2, Chap. 1; WISSLER, *Material Culture of the Blackfoot Indians*, AP, AMNH, V. 5.

[10] See the following besides GRINNELL and WISSLER: DENIG, *Indian Tribes of the Upper Missouri*, RBAE, V. 46; GREGG, *Commerce of the Prairies*; KROEBER, *the Arapaho*, BAMNH, V. 1; MOONEY, *Calendar History of the Kiowa Indians*, RBAE, V. 17.

the economic factor have not been clearly analyzed. Mere reference to the existence of an economic motive in warfare tells us nothing of the relationship of warfare to the economic framework of Plains society. Once it is agreed that such a factor must be considered, the whole gamut of economic activities has to be examined from this relational point of view. It hardly needs to be said that economics in primitive societies, in common with our own, is not only concerned with the question of subsistence but with the manifold bonds between economic structure and social relation.

This same truism must be applied to our study of rank in the Plains. If rank bears no relationship to the basic set of institutions in the society, perplexing questions must inevitably arise. Nor can any type of psychologising, penetrating though it may be, erase these questions which are distinctly sociological in character. The method which would prohibit the dissociation of warfare from the rest of culture would equally prohibit the insulation of rank.

I purpose, in the following pages, to re-examine the interrelationships of rank and warfare and their place in Plains culture. It is my opinion that rank and warfare have been lifted out of their socio-economic context with resulting confusion because that context has been imperfectly understood.

The key to the economic situation in the post-Columbian period in Plains history is the advent of the horse. Error in method and absence of data have accounted for the failure to evaluate properly the importance of the horse in Plains economics, and to understand rank and warfare. In addition analysis of the adhesion of horse-culture to rank and warfare has been hindered. This study attempts another approach and supplies additional materials. The results of the study are largely based on field findings among the Kiowa Indians where I paid special attention to the problems growing out of horse culture, warfare and rank.

I proceed first with a consideration of those economic conditions in the Plains that serve as a background for viewing warfare and rank. I then ask whether patterns of prestige and their modes of attainment can have no deeper roots than have been suggested. Finally, I shall investigate how the ramifications of rank are interwoven with the formal element in the rank-warfare nexus.

II. The Horse in Plains Culture

It is one of those accidents of history that an instrument of Spanish expansion in the New World, the horse, was an important factor in barring further expansion to the same nation.[1] With the introduction of the horse the Plains tribes were immediately strengthened economically and militarily and so aggressive did they become that their subjugation would have proved an almost impossible task for the Spaniards. The horse had come into this region from the Spanish settlements in the Southwest around the beginning of the seventeenth century and in the course of little more than a century was diffused through a large part of the Plains.[2] The southern tribes of Texas and Oklahoma, among them the Comanche, Caddo, Kiowa and Pawnee were probably the first to acquire horses. The northern tribes were not slow to follow in the steps of their southern neighbors and by the middle of the eighteenth century the horse was common among the Plains tribes as far as Saskatchewan. Another line of diffusion on the western margin of the Plains accelerated this movement from south to north. By this route a considerable number of horses

---

[1] In part this barrier was to the advantage of Spain, preventing as it did French expansion in the direction of the southwest and explains why Spanish governors were unwilling to exterminate the tribes of the southern Plains. (See Richardson, R. N., *The Comanche Barrier to South Plains Settlement*, 1933.) It is also interesting to note that the horse never became an important element in the life of the hunting tribes of California. In order to maintain their economic and religious domination of the California Indians, the Spanish missions made them into sedentary agricultural peoples and prohibited the use of the horse except for ploughing and traction. Note Dobrizhoffer, *The Abipones*, V. 1, p. 245, "By a useful edict we took care to prevent the Guaranis from possessing horses, to deprive them of the dangerous opportunity of wandering." A nomadic and marauding economy was not to the best interests of the Spanish Missions and similar regulations were established among the Missions of California and of the Southwest. McLeod, *The American Indian Frontier*, New York, 1928, pp. 111–113.

[2] When I first wrote this paper I had followed Dr. Clark Wissler in attributing the introduction of the horse in the Plains to Coronado and DeSoto, but since then Dr. Francis Haines' excellent article has appeared and I have revised this statement in accordance with his irrefutable logic. Cf. Wissler, *Influence of the Horse in Plains Culture*, American Anthropologist, 1914; Haines, *Where Did the Plains Indians get Their Horses?* AA, ns, V. 40, no. 1, 1938.

passed from the Southwest through the Shoshoni peoples to the Plateau Salish and then east to the northern Plains tribes.[3]

Although horses had been introduced at an early date by the English colonists in the eastern United States, this region never became a great source of horse herds for the Plains Indians. The Southwest was the primary source of large horse herds throughout most of the historic period. Continuous raiding of the Texan and Mexican rancherias had begun sometime in the seventeenth century and persisted until late in the nineteenth century. The depredations in the Southwest increased as the needs of the Indians grew and as the outside markets for horses expanded. Horses were traded by the thousands to the east where the French and the Anglo-American colonists were eager buyers.[4] In addition Mexican traders found their way into a good part of the Plains bringing with them foods, utensils and liquor (which at first were luxuries and later became necessities) and demanded horses in return.

Horse culture developed in the Plains for approximately three hundred years. Those tribes which were not in immediate contact with the richest source of horse herds acquired some by trading with and raiding other tribes and by capturing wild stock. Herds of wild horses were found on the Plains apparently soon after their introduction and spread over the region swiftly, probably following the winter grasses. But the supposition that wild horses ever constituted a primary source of the Indians' herds is unfounded. According to all the evidence, raiding was everywhere the principal method of acquiring horses.[5] There is no reason to suspect that Indian horses bred poorly; nevertheless natural increase of the herds apparently did not satisfy the Indian's needs and he was ever impatient to replenish stock.

---

[3] Teit, The *Salishan Tribes of the Western Plateaus*, Report of Bureau of American Ethnology, 1930, No. 45, p. 327. Haines follows the same view, "The Northward Spread of Horses Among the Plains Indians," American Anthropologist, ns, V. 40, no. 3, 1938.

[4] Athanase de Mezieres asserts that in 1776 the Kiowa and Comanche traded to the French in the East 1,000 horses and the same number of mules. The Wichitas were the intermediaries. H. Bolton, *Athanase de Mezieres and the Louisiana-Texas Frontier*, 1768-1780, 2 Vol., Cleveland, 1914; V. 2, pp. 120-121.

[5] See for example: J. Mooney, *17th Report Bureau of American Ethnology*, V. 17, 1895; Denig, E. T., *Indian Tribes of the Upper Missouri*, 46th Report BAE, 1928, Grinell, G. B., *The Cheyenne Indians*, 2 Vol., Hartford; A. L. Kroeber, *The Arapaho*, Bulletin American Museum of Natural History, V. 1, 1902; Teit, *op. cit.* The peoples of the western Plateaus were for a limited time the only exceptions to this general rule.

Study of the influence of the horse in Plains culture was begun by Wissler[6] in an article which has been regarded as a classic exercise in a method often used by American anthropologists. Turning to a list of characteristic Plains traits which include coup-counting, military societies, the Sun Dance, earth lodges, maize, etc., Wissler finds that they can all be dated as pre-horse. Therefore, the horse could not have induced the development of any of these traits. Wissler does allow that certain minor consequences followed the introduction of the horse, such as the abbreviation of the bow and shield, the decline of pottery and horticulture among the village peoples, and the increase in the extent of movement within the hunting range (although large-scale migrations did not increase). Warfare became more intense and intertribal contact increased. The acceleration of contact and diffusion of typical traits has, in recent times, given rise to the relatively homogeneous culture area in the Plains and constitutes one of the main effects of horse culture. As Wissler summarizes, ". . . only those traits directly associated with the horse, saddle, etc., can be taken as later; the most characteristic traits for want of evidence to the contrary must be given priority and that while the horse along with other European influences may have intensified and more completely diffused the various traits, there is no good evidence at hand to support the view that the horse led to the development of the important traits." In short, ". . . from a qualitative point of view the culture of the Plains would have been much the same without the horse."[7]

It must be remembered that Wissler's study was undertaken in the absence of a great deal of ethnographic data which have further illuminated the problem since then. Yet the basic criticism which can be levelled against this estimate of the rôle of the horse in Plains culture must proceed from his atomistic conception of society. Wissler's analysis regards independent traits most often drawn from the realm of material culture as primary cultural facts. The process of social change means the introduction or disappearance of such traits among a people. The relational factors —the inter-working of traits or institutions, the bonds between

---

[6] WISSLER, 1914, op. cit.
[7] WISSLER, op. cit., 1914, p. 16.

the elements of culture and the positional differences of these elements—are largely ignored. Traits, according to this view, are units which can be plotted on a map to establish the historical connections of tribes and to deduce culture areas. But plotting distributions, tracing diffusions and dating the origin of the various traits hardly replace sociological analysis.

Wissler's thesis that the horse acted as a catalytic agent to intensify certain traits in Plains culture without really participating in the operation is an aspect of the same method. It is a kind of cultural chemistry in which traits may be quantitatively modified without effecting their qualitative nature. Thus, since traits can be intensified without suffering change in their composition and relations, the concept of intensification loses all sociological significance. Crucial as it is to Wissler's argument the concept finally comes to rest on loose and literary ground. When it is applied to warfare, for example, it might mean more war or more destructive war (or could it be a purely psychological description of the feelings of the warriors?)—one is really at a loss to interpret its meaning.[8] In any case it is clear that modification in the intensity of warfare must come as a result of a new factor or series of factors at work in the culture implying changes in institutions and shifts in their relations. Moreover, the end result—more intense warfare—will in turn leave its discernible effects on the culture.

This approach has little in common with the view of traits as discrete elements on the surface of culture.

It would be unfair to expect the horse to bring something with him, as if the animal should at least have had the perspicacity to bring some of the rich forms of social organization common to European feudal and mercantile society. To ask that the horse mechanically develop new traits in the culture is to fail to see that the horse can only "develop" traits as it acts upon existing institutions from which must emerge a changed culture.[9] The invention of the locomotive in our own society likewise has no importance as a developer of traits unless one investigates the rôle of trans-

---

[8] See WISSLER, *op. cit.*, 1914, p. 17.

[9] This is the method which generally guides Lefevre des Noêttes in his *L'attelage et le Cheval de Selle a travers les Ages*, Paris, 1933. Des Noêttes, however, ofttimes becomes oblivious to the complexity of the factors involved and occasionally makes changes in horse gear responsible for the whole course of civilization.

portation in the historical development of our society, the relations of transportation to other phases of culture, and the functioning of the locomotive in the new setting of transportation, in industry and in economic and political expansion. We shall see that the rôle the horse played in the economic life of the Plains people and the extent to which it influenced their culture cannot be exaggerated. Perhaps the most suggestive estimate of the influence of the horse has been given by those American officers who, in trying to crush the Plains Indian and to stamp out his culture, first exterminated his horses.[10]

In order to measure the influence of the horse in Plains culture some data are first needed on the number of horses found among some of the Plains tribes. An indication of relative wealth in horses will in itself set the economic framework of the problem. Moreover, it is not necessary to appeal to abstruse points in natural history to assert that a horse is not a dog and that a herd of horses offers altogether different problems from the packs of dogs which they replaced. Horses need to be herded and pastured and require a certain amount of care and attention that dogs do not receive. Large herds in this way produce a new field of economic activity.

As we have already pointed out there were two centers of great horse wealth in the Plains, the northwestern and southwestern Plains, both in contact with New Spain—the richest source of horses in North America. The Coeur d'Alene and Flathead on the edge of the western Plains were the earliest large scale herders in this general region.[11] According to Teit, about the end of the 18th century the Crow had more horses than the Blackfoot and the Gros Ventre whereas both Shoshoni and Flathead were far wealthier than the Crow. No absolute figures for any of these groups appear in the literature, however, until the beginning of the 19th century by which time the distribution of horses must have been radically changed. The Crow were at this time probably the richest horse owners, and Maximilian gives the figure of 9,000 to 10,000 horses for 400 tipis.[12] Although this figure was reported to Maximilian by informants it need not be skeptically received. The

---

[10] See Mooney, Kiowa Calendar, p. 11.

[11] The Plateau Salish were in a favorable position to increase their herds at first because the Plains tribes did not take to raiding at once. See Teit, op. cit., p. 317.

[12] Maximilian, Travels in North America, V. 1, p. 174.

Crow figure would average some 25 horses per family and though, of course, the horses were not evenly distributed among the family heads of the tribe, the presence of herds based on this family average agrees with other data.[13] Maximilian also recorded suggestive statistics for other tribes. One Blackfoot by the name of Sackomapoh is said to have owned between 4,000 and 5,000 horses and at his death 150 were killed.[14] In another place we find, "Many of the Sioux are rich, and have twenty or more horses . . ."[15] which coincides with Catlin's generalization for the Upper Missouri: "Scarcely a man in these regions is to be found, who is not the owner of one or more of these horses; and in many instances of eight, ten, or even twenty, which he values as his own personal property."[16] Speaking of the Teton specifically, Maximilian states that the rich man owned 30 to 40 horses.[17] Somewhat farther east and especially among the village peoples wealth in horses was not nearly as noticeable. Two Mandan villages, one consisting of 65 huts and another 38 having a joint population of 900 to 1,000 people owned some 300 horses. This meant that a considerable number of individuals had no horses at all.[18] Three Hidatsa villages together had about 300 horses.[19] The Cree had few horses.[20] For the Assiniboine Denig says,[21] "In a large camp at least one-third of the men have no horses that they can catch."[22]

---

[13] "Now this nation (Crow) has from 40 to 80, and sometimes 100 horses to a lodge. . ." DENIG, p. 454.

[14] MAXIMILIAN, *Trends in North America*, V. 1, p. 259.

[15] IBID, V. 1, p. 152.

[16] CATLIN, V. 1, p. 161.

[17] MAXIMILIAN, *op. cit.*, Vol. 1, p. 160.

[18] CATLIN, V. 1, p. 259.

[19] IBID, V. 1, p. 262.

[20] IBID, V. 1, p. 264.

[21] DENIG, *op. cit.*, p. 456.

[22] It should be noted that the western Plateau and Columbia River peoples were early in the possession of fairly large numbers of horses. Before the Blackfoot and Crow had obtained horses they were passed up the Pend d'Oreille and Columbia Rivers to the western Salish and Sahaptin peoples and on to the coast. The Columbia, Colville, Spokan and Nez Perce were well supplied as early as the Coeur d'Alene (TEIT). The peoples at some distance from the waterways were apparently not as fortunate as the river peoples. The Lake had almost no horses because of the unsuitable country. The Sans Poil also seemed to have few horses. (See VERNE RAY, *The Sans Poil and Nespelem*, University of Washington Publications in Anthropology, Dec. 1932, V. 5, p. 117.) Farther west, the Cayuse were very wealthy in horses and supplied the peoples north and south of them. About 1867, Klikitats and Yakamas owned some 10,000 horses (Cong. Rec., Rep. of Com. of I. A., p. 286) which may be taken as an index of the extent of horse wealth in at least a part of the area.

The southwestern Plains, the other great center of horse wealth, must also be considered a source of supply for the southeastern as well as the northern Plains. The Kwahadie bands, those Comanche living in the Staked Plains with a population of less than 2,000, had according to Lorenzo Labadi about 15,000 horses in 1867.[23] The Kiowa, with about 1,500 people, are said to have had 6,000 horses in 1869,[24] a number which by no means is to be regarded as the high point in the size of their herds.[25] Progressing eastward, we find that here too the size of herds dwindles considerably for the village peoples. Dr. Weltfish estimates about 150 horses in a Skiri village with the population of 300. For the year 1867 the RCIA gives for the entire Pawnee tribe 1,400 horses; 1,200 for the Osage; 1,200 for the Omaha. As we have suggested in the case of the northern Plains the greater the distance from Texan and Mexican rancherias, the fewer horses found among the Indian tribes. The southwestern Plains and the western marginal peoples who raided toward the southwest were the richest, while those who were not in direct contact with the original source of horses had to raid neighboring Indian tribes. It seems quite clear that the Indians were better able to defend themselves against raiding than the Mexican ranchers. Thus the coming of the horse to the Plains tribes did not merely entail the addition of a few riding animals to the possessions of a tribe. In many places, at least, the figures of horse wealth indicate the presence of large surpluses. Of the three tribes selected for brief treatment of some major problems connected with horse culture, two of them, the Coeur d'Alene and Kiowa are notable for possessing surpluses. The other, the Pawnee, represent an eastern tribe with a relatively small number of horses.[26] It is not the object of these summaries to deal in detail

---

[23] See RICHARDSON, R. N., p. 310. The Kwahadies had at this time besides horses, 300 or 400 mules, over 1,000 cows and a great number of Texas cattle. Raiding for cattle had become an even better industry than horse raiding in late times. In the case of cattle the Mexicans provided the market and the frontier ranchers the source.

[24] Reports of the Commissioner of Indian Affairs 1869, p. 385.

[25] The decline in the number of horses among the southwestern Plains proceeded steadily during the last half of the 19th century. In 1874, the Kiowa, Comanche, Apache and Delaware had 14,810 horses, and in 1877, 4,194 horses, a reflection of political and economic breakdown. Again in 1880, the Kiowa, Comanche, Apache and Wichita owned some 9,000 horses, but this seeming rehabilitation is a phase of reservation system which does not concern us here.

[26] The Coeur d'Alene data is taken from J. A. TEIT's "*Salishan Tribes of the Plateau.*" The paragraphs bearing on the Pawnee are in part suggested by W. D. STRONG's Introduction to

with the influence of the horse in these three cultures. Only enough data is offered to suggest problems and to illuminate processes.

The Coeur d'Alene are of special interest because, contrary to what seems to have been the general rule with the marginal peoples, they did not come into the Plains until they were already well supplied with horses, and were hence equipped for successful hunting and nomadic life. Actually they were compelled to move to the grasslands from the forested country which was unsuited to horses in order to maintain their herds. Before the introduction of the horse, the Coeur d'Alene were a semi-sedentary people spending most of their time fishing, hunting, root-digging and traveling along the rivers and lakes within their territory. A high development in the art of fishing, canoe making, weaving of mats, bags, and baskets characterized their way of life though there were no truly permanent houses or villages. The first reverberations of the presence of the horse in this area gave a strong impetus to inter-tribal trade, visiting and intermarriage. Trade especially was markedly affected. Larger quantities of meat and fish were transported and great numbers of horses passed from east to west in trade. The trade routes were changed. The introduction of the horse into Salish country meant the abandoning of many of the waterway trade routes for open grassy country suitable for horse travel. Because of the widening of inter-tribal contacts the country inhabited by the Salish was completely opened to influences from the east and Plains traits were rapidly diffused through the region. Tribes such as the Thompson and Shuswap which were hardly exposed to influences from the Plains and Southeast, before the horse, received many Plains traits.

Teit sums up the changes that were gradually realized in the life of the Coeur d'Alene by the introduction of the horse: (the horse) "drew them away from the lakes, and in great measure from fishing, canoes, bark, and wood, materials which they were accustomed to use. They could not follow the old life on the water and in the forests, and at the same time keep horses. Besides, as raising and herding horses and buffalo hunting necessitated much travel, the people had not time for their former industries. Furthermore,

Nebraska Archaeology but are mainly based on DR. WELTFISH's unpublished field notes on Pawnee Economics which she kindly put at my service. The Kiowa data are drawn from my ms. "Kiowa Economics."

many of their utensils were unsuitable for the new style of life. Objects made of wood, bark, and basketry were either too bulky, cumbersome, or fragile; therefore they were largely dispensed with. Bags of skin, leather, and rawhide took the place of basketry and woven bags because they were better suited for travel by horse. Instead of the former small hunting parties, consisting of people of one band or part of a band, hunting now became largely a tribal business, and demanded a different organization. The easier method of making a living offered by buffalo hunting, as well as the pleasure and excitement of traveling and mingling with strangers, which it afforded, were great inducements. Once horses were plentiful, intercourse became easy and general between all members of the tribe, and buffalo hunting as a tribal affair could be engaged in. The old system of chiefs of bands and divisions became obsolete, and only tribal chiefs continued to be recognized. There were really no more bands or divisions. The change from a tribe consisting of many semi-sedentary bands with as many headquarters to a single, almost entirely nomadic community, with a single center, was in time almost completed.[27] The old communal dance houses were abandoned and dancing was conducted entirely in the camp circles."[28] The horse was taken over from the south, but the culture complex which was adopted in consequence was thoroughly Plains. The large nomadic hunting group functioning through nine months of the year, traveling customarily with women, families and pack animals in the center surrounded and protected on all sides by warriors, with scouts before them; the concentration of political control in the hands of tribal chiefs and a Council; and the division of the warriors into companies each with distinct functions—all testify to the attraction of Plains forms of organization for the Coeur d'Alene in their new way of life.

The Coeur d'Alene exemplifies the case of a marginal people unable to adjust the pastoral complex to its former life and compelled to descend onto the Plains there to adopt a more congenial

[27] This change was in part, at least, due to the need for protection against the large-scale raiding activities of the Blackfoot, Crow, etc. The Blackfoot especially were noted for their large war parties.

[28] TEIT, p. 151-152.

existence.[29] On the other hand, in the case of the Pawnee, a partial adjustment to the original (pre-horse) culture seems to have been made at least for the given moment in their history. Tendencies were present which in the long run would perhaps have made the adjustment impossible and might have produced as drastic a change as occurred in Coeur d'Alene society. But as to whether a typical nomadic hunting people would have ultimately emerged is admittedly in the realm of speculation. The advent of the reservation system closed in on whatever direction Pawnee culture was taking.

According to Dr. Weltfish's data there appears to have been some sporadic and casual hunting by the Pawnee in pre-horse times. Antelope and buffalo meat were irregularly obtained to vary the diet of staples obtained from the fields. But the elaborately organized seasonal village hunts were of late origin. The emphasis upon buffalo hunting meant that ". . . in the late period of which Dunbar writes their permanent villages were occupied only long enough to plant and again to harvest the crops."[30] The village was inhabited during March, April, May and half of June and was then deserted for the summer hunt which lasted from the latter half of June through August. The Pawnee returned to the village site in September to leave again for the winter hunt from the middle of December to March. The hunting bands were composed mainly of people who had horses and since the number of horses was by no means evenly distributed throughout the village, the population left behind was not small. In the Skiri village mentioned,[31] with a population of 300 owning 150 horses, about 5 men (chiefs or head medicine men) each owned 9 or 10, a larger group had 4 to 6 horses, a family with 1 or 2 horses was fairly common while half of the people had no horses at all. This is not to say that only half of the village went out to hunt, for a few horses could be borrowed, and some families could join the band on foot, while others hunted near the village or remained around the White settlements.

---

[29] Besides the "pull" to the Plains because of a more secure form of economy there were two direct "pushes", as we have suggested before. First the horse herds were too large to be conveniently maintained in the former Coeur d'Alene habitat. Secondly, the former organization of small bands was unsuited to giving protection against large marauding parties.

[30] STRONG, *Nebraska Archaeology*, p. 298.

[31] See page 11 of this chapter.

Concentration of time and energy on hunting so as to cause the breakdown of the horticultural economy does not seem to have occurred at any point. Planting was always sedulously attended to and, with the exception of those times when the Pawnee suffered at the hands of raiders, there was always sufficient grain stored in pits to satisfy them during the sedentary phase of their life. The Pawnee never seem to have rid themselves of the attitude that meat was a luxury or a delicacy, while the crops were the prerequisites of life. But, though there was no breakdown of horticulture, there was a gradual narrowing of the extent to which it was practiced, a process that was perhaps hardly noticeable at a given moment.

The dual life of a nomadic hunting and a sedentary phase may have already begun in Pawnee pre-horse times but the emphasis on the former became marked after the introduction of the horse. The nomadic hunting activity transformed the older mode of life, and the institutions of the earlier time were altered to include the new activity. Viewing one side of the mutually interactive process, the effect of hunting on sedentary life, impressive data can be especially noted in material culture. Strong's statement that "Few facts are more striking in Pawnee archaeology than the inverse ratio that exists between the abundance of horse remains and the degree of excellence as well as abundance of pottery and other artifacts in such sites"[32] is akin to what we have found for the Coeur d'Alene, with additional significance. It is quite understandable that those handicraft arts which were rendered useless by the nomadic way of life should have quickly fallen away. Among the Coeur d'Alene where transformation was complete the loss was complete also. The Pawnee on the other hand, continued to spend at least half their time in the village. Hence the neglect of the sedentary arts cannot be fully explained unless we consider the possibility that not only were these objects (pottery, basketry, etc.) inappropriate to nomadism but also that in the new economic cycle of the Pawnee the time that had previously been given to their manufacture was now occupied by the hunt.

As for the effects of earlier village institutions on hunting life, they are no less far-reaching. The political organization of the

---

[32] STRONG, *op. cit.*, p. 297.

Pawnee village in pre-horse times conformed to the general principles common to eastern sedentary peoples. A head chief and two or three subchiefs supported by braves comprised the authoritative body in the village.[33] These titles were hereditary with the proviso of validation by exploits in the case of braves, by generous distributions of property in the case of chiefs. The chiefs were the legislative branch of the system, arriving at decisions and commanding the braves to carry them out. The braves were the executors, and though they had no formal right to act as police in the village one of their functions was to maintain peace and order at home. In addition to the braves another class of warriors should be mentioned, the "boys." These differed from the braves in that they were non-political, more fluid in organization, reckless as individuals and without the responsibility of office. The "boys" tended to attach themselves to a chief, performed the routine and undignified tasks of carrying water and procuring wood, and served as the military arm in the defense of the village. There were societies in the village but these were exclusively singing and curing in function.

On the hunt, the form of organization neatly reflected that of the village. The tribal hunt was led and directed by one of the four Pawnee bands. The annual alternation of leadership among these bands was dictated by political considerations; for the Skiri, however, the largest band consisting of four villages, the leading village was chosen by religious sanction. The chiefs of the leading village were in the position of authority, giving direction for movements, and deciding upon questions that arose in the life of the camp. They were assisted in the task of planning camp movements by the "boys" who acted in the capacity of scouts. The braves of all four bands constituted the hunt police while the head brave of the band in charge commanded them. The curing societies were also involved in the transposition of sedentary social structure to the nomadic hunting milieu. As in the case of the other social groups, the functions of these societies were expanded to include the new condition. When the unofficial hunting of small herds at the beginning of the hunting season ceased and the period

---

[33] Each head chief had three braves under him with graded ranks: a head brave, second and third. The subchiefs had one brave.

of sacred hunting opened, the sacred tipi was set up by the leading chief of that season. The power to police the hunt, normally belonging to the braves, was delegated to those bodies which functioned as curing organizations in the village.

Similar modifications are to be seen in the adjustment of the sedentary family organization to hunting life. A village consisted of an aggregate of households, each of which functioned as a social and economic unit. The 10 to 14 residents of the mud lodge usually included three generations of an extended family group and were divided into a North and South side of the lodge. In the northern half, next to the altar on the west, was the position of the young women and their husbands, and immediately east of them were the mature women followed by the grandparents near the doorway. The southern half duplicated the arrangement of the northern half. Elaborate forms of cooperation regulated the life of the members of each group. The North side cooked breakfast; the South side cooked supper. The men of each side helped their side whenever it was called upon to perform a duty. An active mother and daughter composed the cooperative land working unit and when the women of one side were busy with the planting, the other side took over all the cooking. The hunting household unit was necessarily smaller, hardly larger than half of the village household, six or seven. Usually a man and his wife or wives and children occupied one tipi and made up the economic unit. Because they did not provide any real assistance in hunting and because there was a shortage of horses, older people generally stayed behind near the village. In other cases if the three generations, grandparents, parents, and grandchildren, were present in the tipi, the household hunting group did not include the families of the parents' siblings. Another interesting principle determining the composition of the tipi points perhaps to a fundamental change occuring in social organization. Active older women would leave their daughter's village lodge and join their son's tipi for the hunting season and return to the daughter's household again in the village. Apparently the attitude is that in the hunting life the woman is a dependent so that she is more likely to attach herself to her son than remain as a responsibility on her son-in-law. The shift of economic ascendance from women during the sedentary period to men during the hunting period is a striking fact and the mark it left on the village life of the Pawnee opens a significant problem.

The consequences of the horse for Pawnee culture are not exhausted by noting the changes which took place within the society itself. The rôle of the horse among the neighboring peoples must be grasped as well, for, the changes on the outside were far more disastrous for the Pawnee than the modifications of culture within. The arrival on the Plains of nomadic peoples whose predatory habits were strengthened by the possession of horses created great difficulties for the village peoples. The villages were pillaged, the grain pits emptied, and horses were stolen. If any single factor could have forced the Pawnee to give up the settled village life, it would have been the pressure of the nomadic tribes. In any case the Pawnee were on the verge of abandoning their villages. The confined character of settled urban life, plus the almost insoluble problem of sanitation which accompanied it, and the freer social life offered in nomadism made them long for a release from the village. On the other hand, the rich religious and ceremonial life of the Pawnee, which seemed to be the very core of village existence, acted as a powerful force to draw them back to the village each time and halt a permanent exodus. But the fact that the Pawnee were in no position to take on the nomadic hunting complex because of the scarcity of horses among them should be regarded as the most important deterrent.

The Kiowa Indians[34] of the southwestern Plains present a third set of conditions in which the horse played a distinctive rôle. No abrupt change from a horticultural to a hunting economy seems to have occurred for this tribe. They possess no horticultural traditions and before the advent of the horse they must have been a nomadic hunting people. None of the present day Kiowa have any inkling of the fact that Europeans introduced the horse into America. So deeply was the horse imbedded in every phase of Kiowa life that the pre-horse era appears to them as some dark age, quasi legendary. Indeed, the occupation of the Plains by a hunting people without horses is as incredible to the mind of the Kiowa as it is to many students of the Plains area.

The substitution of the horse travois for the travois drawn by

---

[34] For a detailed account of Kiowa horse culture see the writer's ms. "Kiowa Economics."

dogs, the transformation of nomads moving about on foot to a highly mobile people mounted on horses constituted almost an "Industrial Revolution" in the life of the Kiowa. As an historian of this area has pointed out, "The modifications in our own way of living incident to the invention of the steam railway and the automobile were not more far-reaching. . . ."[35] The tempo of life was drastically accelerated, values completely revised. The fluidity of Kiowa bands, which is apparent in the ease and regularity with which individual families changed their band affiliation, the breadth of inter-tribal contact impregnating the culture with new ideas and new material traits, the dependence upon swift and continuous movement for economic success all depended for their development upon the horse. The horse, as a beast of burden and as a riding animal in the service of a nomadic people, effected a new physical adjustment and increased material comforts. Longer tipi poles and more skin covers could be carried which permitted the Indians to live in larger tipis. Preserved food could be transported in sizable quantities and some water. Bows and shields were of necessity abbreviated; the short lance became popular.[36] But in the center of these changes stands the most essential fact, that to the previously impoverished nomads real wealth had been given in the shape of food surpluses, stores of buffalo robes, tipi covers and other objects of value which could for the first time be accumulated in quantities since it could be transported. More than that, the horse became the object of highest value in the culture. The horse industry involving the acquisition of horses, herding, training, lending, and trading became a major industry for the Kiowa.

Although the Kiowa were among the wealthiest people in the Plains, horses were as unevenly divided among the individual members of the tribe as anywhere in the area. Not a few families owned no horses at all, there were many with six to ten horses, well-to-do families owned herds numbering 20 to 50 animals, and a few very rich men could count hundreds of heads in their herds. The horses in a man's herd (or the active part of it if his herd was

---

[35] R. N. Richardson, *The Comanche Barrier to South Plains Settlement*, 1933, p. 26.

[36] These modifications in material culture are strikingly similar to the effects of the introduction of the horse into South America. For example, among the Abipones the short lance came to be used almost exclusively. See Dobrizhoffer, *The Abipones*, V. 1, p. 124.

very large) fell into three classes according to their use and training. The largest group consisted of the transport crew, pack
animals of various types: special carriers of meat, tipis, clothes,
travois pullers, etc. The second group could be classed as saddle
animals ridden by the family; and finally there were a few highly
prized animals exclusively used in the buffalo chase, in military
charges, and for racing. The average household of some five adults
with a well-balanced herd of ideal size owned approximately
ten pack animals, five riding animals and two to five buffalo horses.
With such a herd a family possessed the prerequisites for economic
security and could easily satisfy all its needs.

In a herd of full strength, then, three-fourths of the horses
served for transportation while the remainder was put to use in
hunting and war. This proportion, however, is by no means an
index of the relatively greater importance of the horse in transportation than in the other phases of Kiowa life. The question
of transportation is so intimately bound up with hunting and
warfare that it is impossible to separate the influence of the horse
in one from its influence in the others. Yet the horse's importance
as an agent of transportation is obvious and the effect of placing
the culture "on wheels" is, despite all ramifications, sufficiently
clear-cut. The ability to move quickly over a wide area in order to
follow the migrations of the buffalo gave the Indian a sense of
power. The goodly number of meat parfleches which could be
carried around released them from constant economic pressure and
permitted the enjoyment of a highly developed social life. We
may also suggest in this connection that the frequency with which
people came together in inter-band or intra-tribal contact im-
measurably strengthened political and tribal solidarity.

Although it is unjustifiable to suppose that the horse fulfilled
an important function only in hunting, its importance there
cannot be overestimated. Both the form of hunting and its productivity were affected. As far as Kiowa tradition goes, the surround on foot[37] was perhaps the most striking form of hunt organization in pre-horse times. Stalking buffalo by individual hunters

---

[37] The distribution of types of hunting is very imperfectly known for the Plains and still
less the variations from these types and their relative importance. The surround on foot was
generally achieved by driving the buffalo into a human corral formed by the hunters, women
and children and then making the kill.

was also generally practiced as it was in late times. It is also quite possible that driving the buffalo off cliffs and impounding them in pens[38] were used in pre-horse hunting at some places and times, though the Kiowa remember no such techniques. The favorite method in modern times was the band chase on horseback known as the *akúubɔ*. In this procedure all the available hunters of the band participated with only enough organization to insure that all would ride out at the same time fanwise, without a leader, until they approached the herd, at which moment each man singled out his animal or animals to make his kill. Individual and small party hunts were not uncommon after the advent of the horse, but they were relegated mainly to the winter season. Such small expeditions were usually undertaken to procure fresh meat to vary the preserved meat diet, whereas the semi-organized band chase on horseback which was the dominant form of hunting from spring to late fall provided the staple food supply. The *akúubɔ* did not require an elaborate scheme of cooperation such as the surround; it was not dependent on special topographical features which were necessary for impounding the buffalo from cliffs; and, most important, its informal character permitted the whole band to be held in constant readiness to take quick advantage of the presence of a herd. Among the Kiowa the high productivity of hunting in historic times has been concretely ascertained from an estimate of the amount of meat obtained by the average hunter.[39]

In bringing a new standard of wealth the advent of the horse meant the reorganization of cultural values, for among the Kiowa a man's wealth was counted in terms of the number of horses he owned.[40] Differences in the size of herds were of social and economic consequence. The man with the herd of 100 horses would not necessarily have more than 20 broken horses, the number required for the average family to carry on its basic activities. But the 80 unbroken horses he owned and the insatiable desire to acquire more and more horses was not simply connected with ostentatious display or exhibitionism. The large herd was more than

---

[38] Impounding is perhaps best described in Catlin. See Vol. I, pp. 210-214.

[39] See the writer's ms. "Kiowa Economics," Chapter 3.

[40] *Cf.* RICHARDSON, *op. cit.* The horse was "both a form of capital and a medium of exchange" for the Comanche.

a symbol of the successful warrior and high rank. It meant a man could replenish his active herd from the surplus. It meant a large unbroken herd opened a new source of revenue and provided the means for operating in a new field of economic endeavor—trading. (Among Plains tribes there is a correlation between horse surplus, trading and raiding. These three factors describe a circular course each maintaining and accelerating the other. Thus those tribes that owned surpluses were naturally the most active traders and in turn were compelled to be the most active raiders in order to replenish their surpluses for future trading.)

Related to the Kiowa conception of the horse as wealth is the fact that it became the medium of exchange. In most economic manipulations horses alone or horses plus other items were the principal counters. And even when other objects were included in the trade, horses were considered the tangible and formal objects of value. In trading with the Mexicans for flour, weapons, and ornaments, wild horses were used exclusively. In exchanges between Indian tribes, again it was the horse the Kiowa depended on to uphold their reputation for generosity. In legal adjustments within the tribe horses were chiefly involved. Intra-tribal exchanges were usually made in the form of horses. The services of specialists were paid for in the same medium.

The general processes at work following the introduction of the horse into Plains culture have been roughly suggested for three tribes. The availability of data on horse culture has governed the selection of these particular tribes, materials being too scant to make another selection of tribes practicable. The paucity of rich data bearing on this topic does not reflect on the quality of Plains ethnography as much as it exposes a methodological premise behind much of the work. This premise, which has consciously or unconsciously influenced ethnographic results, contends that if the horse is subtracted from Plains culture as we know it, the residue presents a picture of aboriginal conditions. That the premise has been a spurious guide to Plains researches needs no reiteration. Historical reconstruction in Plains ethnology without reference to the effects of the introduction of the horse can be attempted with as little justification as ignoring the rôle of the machine in the study of social relations in modern society. This is not to imply that the influence of the horse has been equal in weight or identical in form everywhere in the Plains.

Fortunately, the existing facts allow us to study the rôle of the horse under different conditions. The Coeur d'Alene are a marginal tribe who abandoned a semi-sedentary life and took over a nomadic hunting complex as the result of the horse.[41] The Pawnee adopted a dual economic arrangement at the expense of material achievements (pottery, basketry, etc.) and altered the form and function of their institutions. Late Pawnee culture represents a typical adjustment to the horse on the part of a horticultural tribe in the Plains. The Kiowa testify to the influence of the horse on the basic aspects of a traditional nomadic life. The accumulation of wealth in the form of horses by a formerly impoverished hunting people reached extraordinary dimensions here. It has been customary to classify the Kiowa among the other Plains groups under the heading of a hunting economy. The revised view of Plains cultural history challenges this accepted oversimplified classification. For horse pastoralism[42] cut across all lines and forms of the social order and rearranged the economic system with new emphases.

Of the three tribes cursorily explored for the influence of the horse, the last described, the Kiowa, has been selected for intensive treatment of the problem of rank and warfare since field data from this tribe can be brought to bear on the problem. Pastoralism in the Plains was highly developed among the Kiowa so that the economic conditions affecting rank and warfare were strongly marked. The presence of these conditions make special study of the Kiowa case appropriate and advantageous.

---

[41] A good case might be presented to regard the Crow in this same light. Giving Le Raye the benefit of the doubt, at least some of the Crow were living in earth lodges about 1801. According to Teit it was about this time that the western Plains tribes were engaged in wholesale plundering of great horse herds belonging to the Plateau Salish. Hence the coincidence of acquiring large numbers of horses by the Crow and the abandoning of their sedentary life leads me to suspect a causal relationship. See the *Journal of Charles Le Raye—South Dakota Historical Collection*, V. LV, 1908, pp. 172–173.

[42] Plains pastoralism might be defined by the term "nonparasitic" pastoralism to distinguish it from the keeping of herds as a food supply. Hence Plains horse pastoralism is in type similar to the reindeer pastoralism of the Tungus and Yakut in Siberia and unlike the Chuckchee and Koryak who live on their reindeer. Horses were only eaten in emergency in most of the Plains but in some places, notably the Comanche, the horse was a secondary but regular source of food (*a personal communication from Professor Ralph Linton*).

III. The Outline of Kiowa Society

Tradition speaks for Kiowa origin in the north. There is good evidence to suppose that sometime previous to the beginning of the eighteenth century they inhabited the western part of Montana[1] and the Plateau Salish considered both the Kiowa and Comanche members of their western alliance in the struggle against eastern invaders (Blackfoot, Crow, etc.).[2] Linguistic evidence which has been brought to bear on the problem would put the Kiowa language in the Tanoan stock.[3] Whether this might signify a northern origin for the Tanoan speaking people or an ultimate southern origin for the Kiowa it is impossible to determine at present. Further research will have to be undertaken before the problems connected with origins and affiliations are disentangled.

From just before the beginning of the 18th century Kiowa history can be traced in its broad outlines with fair accuracy. Having left the mountains, they first were in contact with the Crow from whom they borrowed the *táime*, or Sun Dance medicine. Apparently mountain country exerted a peculiar attraction for the Kiowa for they drifted into the Black Hills to be later expelled by the incoming Dakota and Cheyenne. They then settled in the Wichita mountains. Pressed southward by overpowering enemies the Kiowa came into contact with the Comanche with whom they were at war until the close of the 18th century. The peace which was finally concluded between these two tribes was lasting and to their mutual profit. Together they raided the Mexican settlements for horses and captives and defended themselves against enemies from the east and west. The Kiowa grew rich. Food in the form of buffalo seemed inexhaustible. The gun was a great boon. Suddenly the bottom dropped out of their seemingly eternal

---

[1] Mooney, *Calendar History of the Kiowa*, RBAE, 17, pt. 1.

[2] Teit, *op. cit.*, p. 114.

[3] Harrington, *On Phonetic and Lexical Resemblances between Kiowa and Tanoan*, Amer. Anthro. v. 12, 1910, pp. 119-123. *Vocabulary of the Kiowa Language*, Bulletin BAE, No. 84, 1928, pt. 1.

security. With the appearance of the agencies of White expansion on the scene, White settlers in large numbers, the military fur and hide companies, railroads, the buffalo began to disappear at a saltatory pace and the tribe was locked within reservation walls.

The Kiowa range in 1832[4] was extensive and strategically situated, particularly for a tribe probably never numbering more than 2,000 members. Bounded on the south by the Wichita mountains and the Canadian River it extended a littler farther north than the Arkansas River and followed its bend in the southeast. The range was well watered and rich in grass lands, altogether ideal horse country. Buffalo migrations cut directly through the heart of this country and antelope and deer were fairly abundant. It lay conveniently near the southwestern trading centers and colonial settlements. The weather was not too rigorous and open winters were the rule.

The economic cycle of this tribe can be divided into four periods. Beginning in late summer and running into December, the Indians spent most of their time preparing for the season of winter inactivity. The tribe was split into some 12 to 15 bands which roamed over the country on the heels of the large buffalo herds, the men going out to hunt every day, the women working at full speed to preserve the meat and tan the hides. In this period a sufficient reserve of food had to be accumulated by midwinter or spring. Raiding parties issued constantly from the camps especially during the first part of the season. Winter saw the largest part of the tribe settled in small relatively stationary camps. Having conveniently dug in along streams sheltered by adjoining wooded land, the Kiowa engaged in almost no organized activity and devoted themselves primarily to social intercourse. Some sporadic and languid individual hunting occurred, but only enough to vary a preserved food diet with a little fresh meat. By spring, food ran low and the bands began to reassemble and resume their movements for hunting. The search for food met with little success at this time because of the seasonal scarcity and poor quality of the buffalo. But the tribe could look forward to improved hunting, an active raiding season, and to the happiest time of the year—the Sun Dance period. The whole tribe convened in midsummer to participate in this

---

[4] See MOONEY, *op. cit.*, map facing p. 140.

social and ceremonial occasion. For a month or two tribal unity was achieved and political solidarity received its foremost and, in fact, its only formal expression. All the normal activities of the band became tribal activities. Religion, of course, became a tribal affair and the ceremony was performed by the various members of the tribe without reference to their band affiliations. Hunting was organized on a large-scale tribal basis under the surveillance of the policing societies. The men's societies met and initiated new members. Old friends and relatives who had not seen one another during the year renewed relations, exchanged anecdotes and threw themselves into the social whirl.

The fundamental social grouping was the band, or *topotóga*.[5] The *topotóga* consisted of an extended family group to which were attached a few families of friends and hangers-on. Preponderant in numbers and dominant politically, the extended family was the nucleus of the *topotóga*. Out of this extended family came the *topotók'i* or headman of the band whose authority sprang from the fact that he was the chief man of the strongest family in the *topotóga*. No system of band authority as such prevailed but the ruling family enforced its regulations on the attached segment of the band as well as on its own members.[6] Actually any kind of compulsion within the *topotóga* was difficult to exert and members of the *topotóga* whether they belonged to the dominant family or not could leave almost at will. The former though were somewhat more restrained since they were subject to the obligations associated with kinship ties. Hence the composition of the *topotóga* was fluid: the frequency with which individual families changed their band affiliations usually for short periods (in the course of visiting friends and relatives) is indeed striking. To apply such terms as exogamy or patrilocality to the *topotóga* adds little to the understanding of the Kiowa situation. Marriage regulations must be generally viewed against the background of political and economic considerations. The extended family group is, of course, an exogamous unit or, in other words, a marrying pair must at least not have had the same grandparents. But the ambition of a

---

[5] The use of the term "band" synonymously with *topotóga* must not be confused with its frequent use in connection with geographical and camp circle divisions.

[6] See the writer's ms. "Kiowa Authority." Cf. also DENIG on the Assiniboine, *op. cit.*

topotók'i was to strengthen the power of his *topotóga* and to increase his following. This could be achieved by members of his own family marrying into the families of unrelated members of his own *topotóga* thereby reinforcing their allegiance. Ideally, every male brought his wife to live in his *topotóga* and every female brought her husband back to her band to increase its size and political supremacy. In practice, the bands maintained a fairly even balance for other factors entered to decide residence. The relative wealth and rank of the two families, parties to the marriage, might be determinative, the poor being attracted to the *topotóga* of the rich. Again, a disproportion in the ratio of the sexes in a particular *topotóga* would have some bearing on the question of residence. On the other hand, the problem of residence might be solved especially in the early stages of a marriage by the young couple dividing its time between the husband's *topotóga* and the wife's. Despite the fact that the most common form of marriage among the Kiowa was elopement, these governing principles were not invalidated.

The *topotóga* operated as a self-contained unit economically, socially, politically and even religiously. It is easy to exaggerate the significance of the Sun Dance in the religious life of the tribe because of its sensational quality and dramatic splendor, but for some ten months of the year the tribe was not together so that religious practice within the *topotóga* must precede in importance its tribal counterpart. Occupying an important place in the life of *topotóga* were the ten sacred medicine bundles. Ordinarily one of them was present in a *topotóga* ministered to by a priest who inherited his office. One of the functions of the ten medicine priests was to adjudicate disputes; they were the bearers of the peace pipes. The bundles themselves were held in highest veneration, the tribesmen displaying the same affect toward the bundles as they did toward the *táime*, the Sun Dance medicine. Sacrifices, vows, petitions were made before the ten medicines not only during the crucial times of a man's life but on any occasion and with regular frequency. In Kiowa life there was much to ask of the bundles and success in war and elevation in rank were by far the most common supplications.

IV. KIOWA WARFARE

There was no inter-band warfare among the Kiowa. Feuds within the tribe sometimes approached dangerously near organized combat though there is no actual case of it. Between tribes, however, warfare was incessant. The generic name for warfare among the Kiowa is *adɔmbánmá*. Employing the root—*dɔmbanmá*, two distinct typeso f warfare are recognized by the addition of prefixes, the *atsĕdɔmbanmá* and the *ak'ataídɔmbánmá*. The former refers specifically to a horse raiding expedition while the latter is used only to denote a revenge party. In addition to a distinction made in terms of the objective of war, another type of native distinction is often used to indicate the direction the war party will take, and prefixes with the same root will name the tribe or locality against which the Kiowa are taking the war path. However, it is the first system of war nomenclature, the one that distinguishes the motivation, which offers a clue to the existence of structural and functional differences in kinds of war parties and, in general, indicates the nature of Kiowa warfare. In native thought war parties are differentiated at every point according to whether they are for horse raiding or for revenge.

The size of a raiding party was from 6 to 10 men. Occasionally 1 or 2 men, perhaps brothers, might go off alone to seek their fortune, and again a large body of warriors, 20 to 30 or more, would sometimes go off for horses. The revenge party, on the other hand, was usually larger. A hundred or 200 warriors was the customary size for such a party although some were smaller. These figures, then, corroborate the principle that raiding parties generally issued from the *topotóga*, that is to say, all the men comprising a war party would belong to the same *topotóga*, while the revenge parties because of their size were tribal in character. The duration of a war party varied roughly with its size. The small raiding parties could stay out almost indefinitely and in some cases a few men were known to be gone for a year or two. Revenge parties were compelled to return in short order so that the other activities of the tribe, mainly hunting, could go on.

From the foregoing it would appear that revenge parties were organized when the whole tribe was assembled and this was usually the case. Immediately after the Sun Dance, as soon as the tabu against going on the war path was lifted, the avenger, who as leader of the expedition must be a prominent warrior though not necessarily a relative, began his preparations. His recruiting campaign was started by sending a pipe to each of the chiefs of the men's societies who, if they approved of the expedition, smoked and presented the pipe to members of their companies.[1] The act of smoking was a sign of joining the party. It is not entirely clear but apparently the society chiefs acted as the adjutants of the leader on the war party, the number of "commanding officers" on a large war party being four. According to Mooney "when a sufficient number have determined upon the expedition, it takes precedence of all others, and no other parties or individuals may start out against the enemy in any direction until this expedition is concluded."[2] In smaller revenge parties which might start out from the *topotóga*, the intention of the leader could be announced by the camp crier and he then had to follow the recruiting pattern of the raiding party which will be described later.

In the expedition for revenge, as soon as the warriors had secured their equipment and fulfilled their religious duties, the company moved forthwith in the direction of a specified enemy. It would appear that in common with many plains tribes, the Kiowa were not enjoined to take revenge upon the tribe responsible for the killing of their warriors. On some revenge expeditions, if the company came upon some other enemy, it would attempt to take a scalp and return home having satisfied its objective. The return of a successful revenge party was always marked by a triumphal entry into the camp. Stopping before the camp,[3] two scouts were sent to ride around it several times and then the column of warriors with blackened faces and in full war dress would ride in shooting their guns into the air, carrying scalps

---

[1] See MOONEY, *Kiowa Calendar*, p. 282.

[2] MOONEY, *ibid.*, p. 282.

[3] Apparently the tribe does not break up finally for the Fall hunting until the large revenge expedition returns since most of the able bodied men participate. The tribe, although strung along in band formation for several miles, would be camped more or less together to receive the returning warriors.

and other trophies flying from poles. Often the women in the camp would come out to meet the returning warriors and climb up behind them on their horses. As soon as they arrived at the center of the camp the drums began and the crowd that had gathered joined in the victory Scalp Dance. The dancing and merrymaking lasted far into the night. Meanwhile, that evening, at an informal council of the older men, the *toyópk'i* might make a report covering the whole enterprise. In the narration of events from the time of starting until the expedition's return, deeds and exploits of particular warriors were recounted in elaborate detail. The cowardly acts were mentioned likewise—who retreated, who pulled up his horse when order for a charge was given. Besides this more dignified meeting, there were spontaneous gatherings in other tipis throughout the camp. A few of the returned warriors were invited to several smaller tipis where they told their stories. When a coup count was recited the women ululated, the audience roared, came to its feet, and danced and sang in the tipi.

The recruiting method followed by a raiding party differs basically from that in the revenge party. Because it was nearly always smaller, its members being usually drawn from a single *topotóga*,[4] and because it had none of the religious aura surrounding the revenge party, there was no formality in recruiting. A pipe was not sent around, but the aspiring leader of such a party first attempted to interest a few friends or relatives in his camp to serve as his assistants[5] and each of these in turn looked about among his own friends to find recruits. A camp crier might announce the intentions of the leader shortly before the appointed time of departure. "On the night before he intends to start, he sits alone in his tipi, having previously bent a long stick, like a hoop, around the fire hole; then he begins the Gua-dagya or travel song, beating time upon the hoop with another stick which he holds in his hand. When those who intend going with him hear the song, they come in one by one and join in it, beating time in the same

---

[4] Raiding parties might start from one *topotóga*, and go to several others in order to increase their size before starting toward their objectives.

[5] There were four captains or *toyópk'i* for a large party, the three *toyóps* subordinate to the actual leader of the party not appearing to be graded. For a smaller party numbering 10 to 12 or more men, there were usually two *toyóps* while in a party of even smaller size there was only one *toyóp*.

way with sticks. The women also come in and sit behind the men, joining in the song but without beating time; after some time the leader invites them to come outside, to a buffalo hide, which the men surround and each holds it up with one hand while they beat time upon it with the sticks. The women and those who cannot reach the hide stand behind and all sing together."[6] The following morning the company took to the war path going deep into Texas or into northern Mexico, the favorite raiding places. It should be noted that both revenge and raiding expeditions left camp on horseback. Sometimes warriors would take a small string of horses, prized running animals, which were ridden only in charges, and pack animals. In the case of surprise raids, the animals were guarded by a few members of the party at a base camp a considerable distance from the point of attack, from which place the warriors proceeded on foot.

The return of a successful raiding party, in common with the return of a revenge party, was met with great rejoicing and was the occasion for celebration. But naturally, one element of the triumphant entry was absent here, the Scalp Dance, unless a killing had incidentally been made on the way or in the course of the raid. On the whole, there was as much singleness of objective in Kiowa war parties as anywhere in the Plains. A revenge party seldom could be turned into a horse stealing enterprise, although capturing an enemy's horse in an attack was certainly not dishonorable. Likewise, a horse raiding expedition would prefer not to engage in combat merely for the sake of combat and scalps.[7] However, fighting was sometimes necessary if the raiders were discovered, or if they were pursued by the victims and compelled to fight their way out. Thus the Scalp Dance and the more formal aspects of the warriors' return tend to become identified with the successful revenge party despite the fact that a raiding party returning with horses and scalps would merit the same reception.[8]

---

[6] MOONEY, op. cit., p. 312.

[7] The ritual before going on the war path also served to distinguish the two types of war parties. "Good medicine" gave one success in raiding; "bad medicine" would enable men successfully to attack the enemy just as a buffalo would stampede into something.

[8] A war party that has had a member killed does not celebrate its return even if it comes with a scalp but all go into mourning and the scalp is sacrificed to the sun by leaving it on some hill. See Mooney, op. cit., p. 291.

The Kiowa do not distinguish between leaders of revenge parties and leaders of raiding parties. But *toyópk'i* who commanded the revenge expeditions must possess greater renown than those in charge of raiding enterprises, since revenge parties ordinarily were of greater dimension, which increased the responsibilities of the leaders. Aside from this the qualifications and functions of the leaders of both types of expeditions were essentially the same. Although the size of a war party varies largely with its objective, within these limits its size depended upon the reputation of its leader who was also its instigator. The success of a war party or its failure nearly always reflected upon the leader. Having failed once, the leader found his following considerably diminished when he next organized a war party. Or a spectacular success in one venture increased his following the next time. Putting the complete burden of responsibility on the *toyópk'i* is comprehensible in the light of two facts. First, his functions took in every phase of the party's activity and secondly, his authority was absolute. The *toyópk'i* selected the camping sites enroute to the war party's destination, he appointed men to stand watch and he himself stood watch all night. He delegated warriors to special tasks, to act as scouts, tend horses, find springs. He decided when they should travel by day and when by night. Even the formation that the warriors used in traveling was dictated by the *toyópk'i*. He performed the religious duties in connection with his own "medicine" on which the whole company depended. If he had prophesying power, he would prophesy the events due on each day for the duration of the expedition. He planned and directed the operations of an attack or raid while he often participated in it himself. In the case of raids, he was in charge of distributing the stolen horses among his followers.[9] The commands of *toyópk'i* were seldom disobeyed. A warrior who did not wish to carry out the orders of his leader sometimes deserted but public opinion would be against him and his desertion might be interpreted as laziness or cowardice.[10] Rarely a *toyópk'i* in charge of an unsuccessful party would resign his office in favor of one of his subordinates. The way in which warriors

---

[9] Seemingly in some cases, after each man on a raiding expedition has obtained one horse, the *toyópk'i* no longer governs distributions, but each man claims whatever horses he seizes.

[10] There were some good reasons for a warrior leaving his expedition and returning home, for example, a serious illness or death in the family.

were sometimes at the mercy of the *toyópk'i* is illustrated in the case
of Tokuléidl. Tokuléidl started out with a small company of about
10 men and after a few days apparently lapsed into some type of
schizophrenic condition, obsessed with the delusion that all of
his men were horses.[11] On one day he stopped the party, lined up
the warriors and examined the teeth of each man. Another day he
forced all of them to bray in chorus threatening to shoot any man
who did not bray or obey him or who deserted. The upshot was
that the party was ambushed and practically exterminated. To
the mind of the informant who reported this case, Tokuléidl had
violated his authority heinously but he was plainly convinced that
little could be done about such cases by the rank and file.[12]

The nature of the *toyópk'i*'s authority in the returning war party
might take several forms according to special circumstances. Normally after a successful or unsuccessful raid, the distribution of
horses having been made and the homeward march begun, the
toyópk'i relinquished his authority and the company was literally
leaderless. If on the way the men were attacked or forced to fight,
any man, not necessarily the *toyópk'i*, could assume the position of
leader. However, in one case I obtained in which a relatively
large expedition seized several hundred horses besides taking a
few scalps, the *toyópk'i* is said to have retained his control for two
reasons: foremost was the fact that the group returned with scalps,
and secondarily so great a number of horses required organized
herding operations. A successful revenge party's return was always
accompanied by the *toyópk'i*'s complete control up to the end of the
Scalp Dance because of the organization attendant upon the triumphant entry. On the other hand a revenge expedition that returned without scalps did not need an active *toyópk'i* for the second
half of its journey. It is not to be inferred from these distinctions
that the returning leaderless war party consisted of a group of
stragglers each taking his own haphazard route toward camp while
the other which continued to be led by a *toyópk'i* acted as a dis-
ciplined cohesive body. Both returns were characterized by a certain amount of informal discipline, self-imposed in the former in-

---

[11] One is led to wonder whether this might be a typical form of psychosis in a culture
in which many individuals are obsessed with the acquisition of horses.

[12] In another case, Gueibóodei who had a tendency to behave quite sadistically toward
his men was only tolerated by his few followers because of his phenomenal success in raids.

stance. Both allowed some individual freedom of action (some of the men hunted along the way; others joined outgoing war parties which they met), but the cohesiveness and integrity of the company, for the most part, was kept intact.

The greater frequency of the raiding party over the revenge expedition displays the predominance of the economic motive in warfare. No absolute figures are procurable. One informant, however, offers an excellent clue when he recalls that as a young and active warrior, he participated in seven raids during one summer. Normally he would not join a revenge expedition but once during the year—the large tribal affair after the Sun Dance. Checking this memory with the experiences of other men leads us to consider the case not atypical. The success of raiding parties seemed to be consistent. Very seldom did a party return with no horses and often a large party would return with as many as a 100 or more horses. A party of 20 men is remembered to have returned with 40 horses. At another time 10 men left the camp to drive back 30 mules which were always desirable. Another analysis of a specific raiding party composed of 19 men showed that 42 horses were taken. In one historic raiding party led by Dohɔ́ɔsɛn, one of the most famous Kiowa war chiefs, 16 men came home with some 300 horses. It is clear in the light of these data, that the basis for the emergence of great wealth distinctions was present.

Raiding in Kiowa society does not come among the controlled activities of the tribe. Nor does it fit into the *topotóga* as such; it is exclusively an individual matter. The attainment of rank among the Kiowa similarly reduces itself to an individual venture. In this way, the problems of rank and wealth of the individual become intertwined.

V. KIOWA RANK

Achieved status in Kiowa society ramified through the whole of the culture and was not limited to the formal type based on military prowess.[1] Special abilities in any sphere of activity were recognized and respected. Medicine men had professional ratings based on their ability as practitioners. Hunters, artists, makers of fine arrows and musical instruments, horse-breakers, herders and native veterinarians were also rated, and the most proficient received the homage of the community and, in the case of the curing profession, obtained considerable economic returns as well.[2] But to compare this social standing with the kind related to war honors is analogous to setting intellectual distinction against financial achievement in our own society.[3]

The formal rank hierarchy of the Kiowa consisted of four categories:

1. *ɔ́ngop*—*Ɔ́ndeidɔ*—a person belonging to this grade. *Ɔ́ndeipadw*—a camp composed of people of this grade. The word *ɔngop* literally means, "fine, distinguished, perfect, best".
2. *Ɔ́ndeigúp'a*—second to ondei, "second best."
3. *Kɔ́ɔn. Kɔ́ɔnk'i*—person, *Kɔ́ɔndɔ*—camp. *Kɔ́ɔn* means poor, propertyless.
4. *Dapóm. Dapómk'i*—person. *Dapómdɔ*—camp. *Dapóm* is used to mean useless, helpless, even criminal. It may perhaps best be defined by the German "Lumpen."

There is a question whether the last, *dapom*, is a special grade in the system of rank at all since it is so frequently used as an epithet. Some informants would class the third and last together. Captives, too, may be viewed apart from this classification but will be considered in relation to the general problem of rank.

---

[1] See appendix to Kiowa Rank. Besides warriors and headmen appearing in the list of the 25 most eminent men of the tribe, some were known for good looks, for ability as orators, horse-racers, lovers, etc.

[2] Some of the best Kiowa cureceivedrers as many as 10 to 12 horses a year for their services.

[3] LOWIE, *Primitive Society*, p. 356.

There are five prerequisites for *ongop* grade. Every *ondeidɔ* should possess good looks. "He should be handsome on a horse." He should have property enough to validate his rank by distributing it when necessary. He should be generous. He must be aristocratic in his bearing and courteous. Above all else, he must have distinguished himself in war. This last overweighs the other four taken together and suggests the fundamental difference between the first and second grade. The *ondeidɔ*'s noble countenance might suffer in comparison with that of his horse. He might have only a few horses and be generous with the property of others. He might even be as boorish as a *dapomk'i*, yet if he held the requisite war record his rank of *ongop* would be grudingly recognized. All *topotoki* (headmen) belonged to *ongop* as did most *toyopki* (war chiefs). A few *toyopki*, however, fell into the second grade. The chiefs of the men's societies were always *ondeidɔ*.

The *ondeigupa*, the second grade, consists of those persons with wealth, generosity, noble personality traits, everything but the war deeds necessary for *ongop* to their credit. Their wealth can never buy them into the aristocracy. Most medicine men were *ondeigupa* as were able hunters, artists, herders, and other nonmilitary specialists unless they were great warriors in addition.

Of the *kɔɔn*, the Kiowa say, "They are also human. They will always be here."[4] The *kɔɔn* were without military achievement or economic independence. Most of the time they were forced to remain attached to their more fortunate relatives from whom they borrowed horses to hunt and for transportation and in exchange performed certain duties in the household of their benefactors. They persistently tried to raise their rank in the face of curtailed opportunities. The *dapom*, the lowest class, had not the sincerity and honesty of the *kɔɔn*. The former would steal from their own kin. They were shiftless and lazy. Their own relatives had practically disowned them and they were virtual outcasts. Usually they managed to live by becoming retainers to the wealthy in whose households they had no more status than captives. The headman regarded a *dapomk'i* as a general nuisance in his camp but had no authority to expel him. He could not punish him if he

---

[4] The Kiowa phrase goes: *kɔndɔ adlgatɔnsadg'* —literally, "The poor are also allowed." *ɔngó ḳatkónb ɔadɔ* "They are our own people."

stole from anyone in the camp. The *dapomk'i* could only be gotten rid of by refusing him economic support, by his relatives' repudiating and shaming him.

These grades were not sharply demarcated; there was a gradual shading of one into the other and there were gradations within each. Members of the same grade occasionally quarrelled over their relative position or over some other person who claimed membership in their grade. In these quarrels all the heroic deeds a man had performed were called up, coup counts were mentioned, the number of enemies killed, and scalps taken were counted, etc. After the disputants had finished recounting deeds and adding up war scores without reaching a satisfactory conclusion, they compared the property owned, the number of captives each had and often their prowess in love. All in all, there was little wrangling about relative status because the community was well aware of every warrior's record. Reports from returning war parties together with the many institutionalized forms of publicity and repeated discussions of military exploits served to give each warrior a fairly definite rating in the scheme of rank.

Kiowa society has been in a non-functioning state too long to make. practicable a careful analysis of how the tribal population was divided according to the four grades of rank. A crude attempt was made by me to obtain an estimate in percentages by teaching the informant to consider the tribe as consisting of ten sticks. One informant estimated the numerical strength of *ɔngop* at 10%, *ondeigupa* 40%, *Kɔɔn* 40% and *dapom* 10%. Another informant put *ɔngop* at 30%, *ondeigupa* 50%, *kɔɔn* 10% and *dapom* and captives 10%. Assuming that the two informants had complete control of fraction operations, the disparity between the two estimates is probably to be explained as a confusion of different historical periods. The political breakdown of Kiowa society accompanied by the destruction of the war complex in the latter half of the 19th century left its disturbing mark on rank. The transition occurred so swiftly and rank was affected so drastically that some confusion in the minds of the informants on this topic would be inevitable.

At the root of rank differentiation was war and all physically fit Kiowa males strove to achieve military distinction. For not only were they dominated by the pressure of the manly ideals in the culture but their economic well-being was at stake. Horses

which were indispensable to economic life were principally acquired through war. However, success in military achievement was
not given to all men and there were those who participated in war
activity in the normal course of performing their regular duties,
refusing or unable to emphasize it above all else. For others, success in war was all-important and to these men who looked upon
war as a career to be followed assiduously the attainment of high
rank was the goal. The young warrior who aimed at *ongop* had to
climb the ladder slowly. He had first to be known as a *kataiki*,[5] a
brave who had seen action and come away with distinction. Having begun his war life at the age of 15 or 16 he might become a
kataiki before he was twenty or sometimes by a heroic performance
on his first expedition.[6] A young man who was just starting his
war career behaved in an extremely exhibitionistic manner in
battle, yelling, running up and charging the enemy spectacularly,
and dashing into every fray. With his first achievements in war
his membership in the men's society usually changed. As an un-
distinguished young man he might belong to the *Adltoyui* company
but after he had won his chevrons he was invited to join one of
the higher ranking societies.[7] There followed a period of intense
war activity in which the young *kataiki* gained ever greater recognition until he became a tribal figure.[8] If his abilities were outstanding he might become a *toyopki*, a war party leader, in his
early thirties. He would first lead small raiding parties composed,
perhaps, of two or three friends or relatives. As his success and
prestige increased he would lead larger and larger expeditions until
he was recognized.

The *kataisopan*, great *kataiki*, is a somewhat formal title applied
to those warriors who have at least four heroic deeds to their
credit and have also taken part in all types of war experience. The

---

[5] A change of name was usually made when a man had reached the *Kataiki* grade.

[6] No one was allowed to vow a Sun Dance unless he had at least the rating of a *Kataiki*.

[7] Kiowa societies were roughly graded according to age and achievement. All the men of
ordinary families usually enter *Adltoyui* first with the exception of the favored sons of wealthy
families. The latter are brought into any of the older men's groups immediately, by which
the members of the society profit. The father of a favored boy regularly distributes goods
to the society membership in honor of his son.

[8] After the "Buffalo Stampede" which is one of the ceremonies of the first day of the Sun
Dance, four *kataiki* were selected by one of the ten medicine keepers to be "knighted." The
ritual formula which is recited while they are being touched with a stick goes: "This is a
young or fat (depending on the man's age) buffalo. His name is so-and-so. Our people can
call upon him on any occasion to do us service. He is a real *kataiki*."

individual does not always focus his attention on the performance of the most heroic deeds but tries to acquire varied experience. The latter is especially looked for in the *toyopki*, who must guard the safety of his men and be capable of coping with any military situation. Versatility of achievement counts in a war score as well as the quality of achievement. Among the Kiowa there is a code of military achievement consisting of a series of deeds some of which have higher value than others. The accomplishment of deeds bearing the highest value, four being the minimum, gives a warrior the rating of *kataisopan*. He then is eligible for membership in the *KoitsEnka*, the honorific men's society, which is limited to a small number of the greatest warriors. It would be entirely misleading to attribute greater formality and schematization to the rating of deeds among the Kiowa than what seems to exist in the Plains generally. Not every deed has its own special value, graded differently in each case; at best there is only a crude grouping of deeds, all the deeds belonging to one group giving approximately the same honor while one group takes precedence over the other. The credit-bearing deeds in Kiowa were:

Group I
1. Counting first coup.
2. Charging the enemy while party is in retreat, thereby covering retreat.
3. Rescuing a comrade while party is retreating before a charging enemy.
4. Charging the leading man of the enemy alone before the parties have met (which is tantamount to suicide).

Group II
5. Killing enemy.
6. Counting second coup.
7. Receiving wound in an honorable action (hand-to-hand combat).

Group III
8. Dismounting, turning pony loose and fighting on foot.
9. Counting third and fourth coup.
10. Serving as *toyopki* often.
11. Success in stealing horses.
12. Efficiency in war camp life (obeying orders, good scouting, etc.).

The four deeds listed under Group I have more or less equal value, and similarly the three subsumed under Group II and the six in Group III. The three groups have been listed in the order of the honor they give, the performance of any of the acts in Group I giving superior status to those of Group II, and the acts of Group I are held in higher esteem than the more prosaic accomplishments in Group III.

The warrior who has been successful in accomplishing certain heroic acts must capitalize upon them immediately. He does not automatically attain the rating of a *kataisopan* by merely performing his deeds and then modestly belittling them or refusing to speak of them at all. Extensive publicity of his attainments is essential and recognition of his attainments must be tribal in scope. Unless a warrior has his deeds on the lips of every member of the tribe he cannot become the great *toyopki* followed by hundreds of men when he announces his intention to go on the war path. It must be remembered that our classification of deeds is after all an abstraction, for in the Kiowa view of this matter, notwithstanding the equal rating of certain deeds every deed was somehow different. Each had its own particular twist of detail; each had its distinctive color and the populace gloried in the recitation of any military experience despite endless repetition. Even the trite recitation of a coup count excited the camp.

The advertisement of military achievement took place in the *topotoga* but primarily in the Sun Dance tribal camp, both formally and informally. The most popular place for the warriors to acquaint each other with their war records was the men's society meetings.[9] At these meetings the members recounted their deeds and counted coup to the accompaniment of drumming, yelling and dancing. Likewise in the dancing outside the societies' tipis the shouting of coups were a regular part of the festivity. There were special forms of recognition accorded warriors who had performed specific types of heroism. For example, the *Tonkonga* society, one of the more important men's societies, gave those men who had turned back from a retreat to charge the enemy an opportunity to narrate their experience. The man who had horses stolen from him and was able to recover them was eligible for the position of

---

[9] Any *Kataiki* can recite his coup counts at the *Polayi* (boys' Rabbit Society) meetings.

caretaker of the fire in the Sun Dance lodge. Those *kataisopan* who had counted coup on Indian enemies recited their coups in the dedication ceremony at the opening of the Sun Dance. *Kataisopan* were also publicly honored in the Buffalo Dances which occurred before and after the Sun Dance. In much the same way they received recognition in the Tail Medicine dances—during both of which they formally recited coups.

Perhaps the most effective manner of publicizing deeds because it is more spontaneous and direct revolves around kinship ties. Especially at the beginning of his career the young warrior is dependent upon his relatives to give him a "build-up." A fond father will do all in his power to see that his son's name and reputation as a warrior becomes widely known. He will distribute property and give feasts in his son's honor. When the young man returns from a successful war party his father will take his relatives and ride around the camp calling out the boy's name as a tested brave. He will sponsor the council meetings that are held at the return of a war party to hear the *toyopki*'s report so that credit may reflect upon his son.[10] He will provide him with his own tipi and with the means to entertain his friends. Although a father cannot recite his son's coup counts in public gatherings he can boost him in countless other ways, enhance his popularity and groom him to occupy a high place in the tribe.

Publicity and possession of military attainments combined to determine the selection of the incumbents of political office. Only the *toyopki* of the highest caliber were eligible to be headmen—*topotokis*. As far as the holding of formal office was concerned, gaining a "topotokiship" was the end of the road for the career warrior. He could rise no higher though he might enter into competition for status with other *topotokis* among whom gradations in position were recognized.[11] Besides publicity and war record, the politically ambitious warrior had to have a fairly large, cohesive

---

[10] See Kiowa Warfare, Chap. IV.

[11] Informants classified headmen on the basis of several criteria: size of camp, having influence with the Whites, and principally war record. Frank Gibbon, one of the oldest of the Kiowa informants, after giving a list of 24 *topotokis*, taken over a period of two generations, classified them as follows: only two were first class, one was probably the greatest warrior of the tribe, Seitägai, who was also chief of the *KoitsEnka*, the warriors honorary society, and the other was Ɔnsoḳaptɔ, the *taime*keeper and also a prominent warrior, thirteen were second class and nine third class.

and wealthy family behind him—one that would follow his rule and support him in fulfilling his economic responsibilities. The *topotoki* was the father of his band feeding all hungry mouths and liberally distributing his property to the needy.[12] To maintain a *topotoki*'s reputation for generosity his relatives had to present him with part of the spoils they had taken in raids. Family support, publicity, war record and political office—all four factors were interrelated.

As we have previously intimated not every tribesman could avail himself of the opportunity for using this mechanism for attaining rank. The non-Kiowa section of the population was completely ruled out of *ongop*. The place of captives in the society deserves special attention. Taking captives is evidently an old and well-established pattern among the Kiowa. Not only were there Mexican captives, who comprised the bulk of the captive population, but there were others of Pawnee, Osage, and Ute origin. Any enemy tribe was a legitimate source of captives. Many were bought from the Comanche who carried on an extensive trade in captives and in their numerous raids into Mexico oftentimes seized Mexican children in preference to horses. Not so the Kiowa. They never sold captives and nearly always concentrated on horses in raiding. Captives were procured mainly when there was a special need for them in camp: some childless woman wishing to adopt a child; or a helper being required for household work.

Only women and children were taken as captives, never men. Men would have attempted to escape while women seldom were so bold; children were ideal, for memories of their homes and families were soon effaced and in time they were assimilated. Sex preference depended upon the needs and wishes of the individual families adopting the captives, and there were approximately as many females as males. It was impossible to obtain an accurate count of the number of captives in the tribe but White Fox (one of the informant) estimated them at five percent.[13]

Captives were not entirely excluded from the system of rank. They never could become *ondeido*, but they could improve their

---

[12] *Topotokis* were not the richest men in the tribe; they seldom owned more than 50 to 60 horses.

[13] There were seldom more than one or two captives taken on any raid, if any at all; never more than three.

status by proving their reliability and efficiency in the service of their masters and by achievement in war. Yet the social status held by captives was the lowest. To their perpetual embarrassment they could never be completely accepted into the culture; it was never forgotten that they were of foreign blood.[14] The first words used by a Kiowa quarreling with a captive were "You are only a captive," as if to say "Know your place." Viewing the relationship from the other side, we learn from Kúitõ, the son of captives, that the full bloods were a decadent, lazy, ineffectual lot, lacking the initiative of the captive in hunting, war and general camp life. "Even today," he asserted, "the mixed bloods are more prosperous, have better and cleaner homes, are more dependable." This unrespected and unrespecting group was put to work at menial and routine occupations and contributed largely toward the welfare of the tribe. I first associated the taking of captives with the tribe's overconscious feeling of its small size and fear that its numbers would be too quickly decimated by war. But this idea is belied by Kiowa practice. Though the Kiowa show a curious inferiority complex regarding their numbers, probably impressed upon them by defeats at the hands of the Dakota, Cheyenne and Comanche, the Kiowa chose to employ the captives as workers, not as warrior recruits.

As small boys, the captives carried water, hauled wood and took care of the smaller children. A little later they became horse herders. As young men they did much of the hunting besides the herding. They became expert horse breakers. If they were taken on war parties, they were compelled to do the drudgery, attending to camp duties, cooking, etc. They could participate in battles but naturally had fewer opportunities to distinguish themselves. Both the men and women captives did a considerable amount of butchering. Women looked after the household work as helpers of their mistresses. They performed the menial work, cared for the children, helped in tanning and food preserving.

The treatment of captives differed depending on the particular relationship of each to the persons of his household. A few were received into the family as adopted children and were not over-

[14] Mɔkín, a Mexican captive, was adopted by the *taime*keeper and was taught the ritual. He took an important part in the Sun Dance itself but never became the actual *taime*keeper.

burdened with work. They were given good names and could inherit some property from their foster parents. The non-adopted were usually given ludicrous names (if they had any physical deformity or marked physical characteristic, their names would call attention to it), and were taken as servants from the very beginning. Intermarriage between captives and full bloods was not infrequent but there was a stigma attached to it for the full bloods who might suffer ridicule. Captives seldom intermarried with prominent families but if the foster parents of an adopted captive were well-to-do they would try to make a good match for him. Non-adopted captives often married among themselves and then both husband and wife would work for the same family. Or a poor family seeing that some captive was an able worker would try to marry a daughter to him in the hope that he would help mend their fortune. There would be no gifts exchanged between the girl's family and the captive's.

Generally speaking captives were not treated cruelly or abused. Only when a man brought home a captive wife to live with his Kiowa wife did the latter sometimes maltreat the captive, who might be overworked and beaten. Even non-adopted captives were often generously dealt with. Big Bow once took a Mexican captive by the name of Kuitan with him on a war party. Kuitan acted as a personal servant to Big Bow on this expedition, cooked for him and took care of his horse. When the party seized thirty horses, Big Bow who was to divide them in his capacity as the *toyopki*, let Kuitan have the first choice. The warriors grumbled a little at bestowing this honor upon a captive but Big Bow had his way. A wealthy man might also show his fondness for his captive by equipping him with a horse and other necessary war accoutrements and allowing him to go off on a raiding party. If the captive secured a few horses he would present one or two to his master. However his way in gaining prestige lay more conveniently in the direction of competent performance of camp duties for which he might occasionally be given a horse by his master until, in some cases, he acquired a herd of respectable size. These horses were the captive's own personal property and could not be commandeered by the owner of the captive. It would be erroneous to consider Kiowa captives in the same class with slaves. Many of them were bought, it is true, but they were not regarded as property. Most of them were taken in their childhood to grow up as Kiowa which made their amalgamation with the tribe and their membership in a family quite real. The possibility of a captive running away from his master or foster parents was hardly conceivable. He was tied to his family group as was any dependent of Kiowa blood and once he broke this tie he fell into the class of *dapom* creatures. Though it would seem that captives occupied a position in the family akin to poor relatives because they were ineligible for some offices and could not use certain medicines, they must be put a step lower than the *Kɔɔn* in the social scale.

The limitations of opportunity for the *Kɔɔnki* to traverse the prescribed road to high rank is defined in his dependence upon his rich relatives. Rarely having buffalo horses for hunting and usually lacking sufficient horses for transportation, the *kɔɔn* were obliged to borrow from the *ɔngop*. To borrow horses they had to follow their more fortunate relatives, thus losing some of their freedom of movement; the *topotoga* to which they belonged at any particular time depended upon the affiliations of their wealthier kin. In return for their kindnesses the wealthy demanded certain services of the *kɔɔn*. At times the latter were expected to hunt for their benefactors or turn over a part of their kill as well as spend considerable time herding horses for them. A typical case is the one of the *ondeidɔ* who needed hides for a new tipi but was anxious to go on a raid. To satisfy himself on both scores, he lent five buffalo horses to poor relatives with the arrangement that they keep all the meat and give him all the hides. In this way he obtained ten hides in one day and was able to depart immediately on his raiding venture.

A young *kɔɔnki*'s rise to fame must follow a slow and tortuous process. If he is ambitious and strives to make his mark, he may borrow a horse from a rich relative and outfit himself to accompany a war party. To compress the career of a model *kɔɔn*, on this his first expedition, he may bring back two horses in addition to the borrowed one. He returns his relative's animal and also gives him one of the two horses he took in the raid. The *ondeidɔ* has made a good investment and the young man has his own horse. Perhaps the *kɔɔnki*'s next venture will net him three horses, a third raid may bring his capital up to six or seven horses. His family has begun to be independent and from then on it will be able to control its own movements and hunt without having to borrow horses. More raids may add two or three riding horses and some wild mares and mules to his stock. He has now "climbed out of the bush of *koon*" as the Kiowa put it. Several years of raiding and breeding may have brought his stock up to twenty or thirty head and people speak of him with respect. He is a wealthy man and as he rises in the world he will present his rich relatives and former benefactors with a horse or two at regular intervals.

To continue his ascent to *ongop* is another matter. The acquisition of wealth and the achievement of independence has been his main concern during most of his active life. In contrast to an *ondei* son he has had to think first of economic returns and secondarily of brave deeds, of coup counts. He has not deliberately avoided combat whenever it was thrust in his way or conducted himself dishonorably in any military maneuver, but rather his deeply impressed economic needs have made him less disposed to push himself forward and seize the opportunity to perform a deed. To phrase it in another way, his reaction time in reference to performing formal deeds is considerably slower than that of an *ondei* son. Given a situation in which an enemy has fallen from horse, the young *koonki* is torn between counting coup and riding after the enemy's horse. The rich man's decision is much simpler; he counts coup. Furthermore the young *koonki* has been inclined to follow those *toyopki* who were themselves primarily interested in the economic fruits of war. In addition to this emphasis upon raiding, the *koonki's* attainment of *ongop* rank is made difficult in another way: manipulation of publicity is essentially in the hands of the rich and in the absence of publicity the deeds that the *koonki* has accomplished are without substance or significance. Thus unless a young *koon* has been fortunate enough to win an *ondei* sponsor, let us say a wealthy childless uncle, to relieve him of burdensome camp duties, to throw opportunities in his way, and to use his means to support him, *ongop* is almost beyond his reach.

The enhancement of opportunities to achieve *ongop* rank among the rich now stands out in sharp relief. The result of the division of labor by rank freed the young man of *ondei* family from some of the unheroic drudgery of hunting and herding. High rank did not rigidly define a man's occupations; every man hunted and devoted a portion of his time to herding, every man made bows and arrows and participated to some extent in war. But the *ɔngop* who possessed poor dependent relatives and captives to help them could free their sons to pursue war careers. Concentrating on achieving a high war score the *ondei* sons of ability could rise quickly to their fathers' rank.[15] Desire for booty could for the moment remain unemphasized. This is not to say that the *ondei* had no economic interest in warfare. The rising *ondei* whose desire it was to be a *toyopki* must be a specialist in horse raiding as well as a brave fighter. For him, active and successful participation in war meant lucrative profit in horses throughout his career. In the end the system was set for the polarization of wealth; those who already possessed it had greater opportunities to engage in the wealth producing occupation.

It might be supposed that on the basis of the functioning of wealth in Kiowa rank, the perpetuation of rank within an *ondei* family would be almost automatic. Such was not the case. Despite all their advantages many men of *ondei* families never arrived and had to be satisfied to be known as sons of *ondeidɔ*, belonging to the second or third grade.[16] According to Kuito, about 30% of the sons of *ondei* become *ondei*, another 40% become members of the second grade, the remainder drop to third or fourth.

The rank of woman approximates more nearly an hereditary pattern. It reflects the rank of their fathers and secondarily of their husbands.[17] The daughter of an *ondei* remains *ondei* even if she marries beneath her rank. In this case she does not rank as high as the *ondei* woman who has married an *ondei* man, but the rank of her family influences others to treat her with respect. Ideally *ondei* women should be virtuous, wealthy and beautiful. Thus if a beautiful woman whose family is *kɔɔn* marries an *ondei* husband and proves to be a faithful wife, and if she accumulates property

---

[15] The *ondei* father in taking pains to have his son emulate him, instructed him in the moral qualities he would need as a warrior. He impressed his son with the precept that it was better to die in battle than to die a natural death. He told him that he would not feel brave every day but to take advantage of those days when his heart was brave and not disgrace himself on the others.

[16] The second generation of an *ondei* family might still retain its wealth and thereby accelerate the rise of the third generation to *ɔngop*. The frequency of skipping a generation however, could not be investigated.

[17] See Appendix. All of the eminent women were *ondei* with the exception of those whose husbands were not *ondei*.

in her own right, she ascends the scale of rank. She will be considered *ondei* even if born *ondei* women snub her. On the other hand, "crazy" (promiscuous) girls of *ondei* families become *dapom* creatures.

The attitude of one ranking group toward another must be examined first as they affected the kin group. On the surface, the kin group was unified and cohesive. Ties of kinship served as a strong inducement for the rich to assist their *kɔɔn* relatives and the reciprocating services of the *kɔɔn* were embodied in the kinship obligations and were not put in the category of paid labor. Likewise in the feud situation *kɔɔn* and *ɔngop* stood behind each other. Yet native accounts make it clear that property distinctions within the kin group acted to break up its unity in some measure. There are many tales of rich men refusing to aid their poor relatives. Whether these cases increased proportionately to the increase in wealth differences is only a matter for speculation. The rich who behaved toward the poor in this way were frowned upon, were immoral according to Kiowa standards, but that kind of immorality seems to have been an inevitable outgrowth of the situation.

Where a rich family and a *kɔɔn* family belonged to different kin groups, an undercurrent of antipathy between them found expression in the phenomenon of "outfacing." Connected with rising in rank, outfacing an *ondeidɔ* can be conceived of as a type of military achievement. This is often accomplished by stealing the wife of an *ondeidɔ*. The case of Kúitotai vs. Seitoyóitɛ illustrates the pattern neatly. K, an orphan, began his life as *kɔɔn* but at an early age made a name for himself in war and became a *toyopki*. Despite the fact that he was a first-class warrior and had accumulated a sizable herd of horses and dressed well, some people did not consider him a true *ondeidɔ* because of his humble origin. One year while he was camping in the north he decided to elope with the wife of Seitoyóitɛ, one of the tribe's principal *topotoki*. He carried out his plan without difficulty and took her with him on a raiding party. S organized a party to pursue him but after an unsuccessful search of several days he returned still plotting revenge. K soon after returned with the woman. S caught him alone one day and sent an arrow under K's shoulder. He searched out his wife and tried to cut off her nose but only succeeded in slitting it. After K was cured of his wound by the buffalo doctors, he sent a ten-medicine priest with a pipe to S in order to make peace. S accepted the pipe, took back his wife, adopted K as his brother and the matter was closed. A little later K eloped with the same woman a second time returning several years later, after S had been killed. By stealing the wife of a great chief as well as by his other accomplishments, K had earned for himself the indisputable title of *ondeidɔ*. By stealing her the second time he displayed the height of courage which made him almost a hero.

Those who had fought their way up to *ɔngop* from the lower grades did not entirely lose the stigma of the newly arrived. Their *ɔngop* position remained somewhat insecure no matter how distinguished their war record might be. The *ondei* sons of *ondei* fathers might have been inferior in their accomplishments to the first generation but their rank was nevertheless more exalted. The "good" families had a tendency to become crystallized and enclose themselves in the atmosphere of caste.

Caste attitudes are to be seen in the *ondei*'s conception of the use of medicine for elevating one's rank. A man on his first or perhaps second war party will carry no shield but after his first experience in fighting he will look about for a shield which has supernatural protective power. He can obtain a shield in two ways: either by going out for a vision in which a spirit will tell him how to paint his shield, on what side to carry it, when to take it out of its case, its tabus, how to make its power efficacious; or he may buy a shield, learning from the owner how to use it. Any number of replicas of shields can be made unless the number is specified in the original vision. Occasionally one may also receive a shield from a close relative as a loan during a probation period. If the borrower performs some brave deed during that time the shield is his, and if he fails he must return it. Viewing the tribe as a whole, many men in all ranks had medicine shields or bundles. About three fourths of the *ondeidɔ*s possesses medicine and about one half of the others. However one side of the *ondeidɔ*'s attitude toward medicine is well illustrated by those men of high rank who were not owners of medicine. The Kiowa recognize that bravery depended upon the man and not on his supernatural power; medicine protected the man but could not transform the coward into a brave warrior. Disregarding any need for protection, some *ondeidɔ* considered it a sign of sublime courage to go entirely with-

out medicine of the personal sort though they of course participated in the more social religious observances (10 medicine pledges
for example) which may influence the success or failure of a war
expedition. In harmony with the upper caste prejudice of stressing
the limitations of personal medicine and regarding its acquisition
a formal matter to be indifferently pursued, most *ondeidɔ* bought
their medicine. They could afford to take the short cut and generally leave the visions to the lower classes. For the young braves
of the poor whose ambition was to become *ondei*, the inspiration
and security of a vision were imperative and one of the first steps
toward making a career.

Other characteristics which are attributed to *ɔngop* differentiat-
ing them from the bulk of the population in subtle ways are reflected in the following two anecdotes:

Gúseibai, a Comanche, living among the Kiowa married a
Kiowa woman of *ondei* rank. Her relatives were not sure of G's
rank. They decided to test him. The plan was to sing a Sun Dance
song and if he succumbed to the rhythm and moved his arms and
legs in time with the music he was certain to be of low rank.
One night some relatives of his wife came over to his tipi and began
to sing a Sun Dance song. At first the Comanche lay motionless
but soon his body was swaying and his feet were keeping time.
That was enough. They were sure he was *dapom*. An *ondei* must
exercise restraint at all times and never exhibit his emotions.

A young man of marriageable age whose father urged him to
get a wife eloped with an *ondei* girl and brought her back to his
father's tipi. She was beautiful and accomplished. The young
man's father in order to test the girl asked her to cook him some
meat which she did very meticulously, using a clean grate and
carefully selected coals. But the father was not satisfied. He told
his son to return the girl to her parents. Again the son brought a
beautiful *ondei* girl home. Again the father tested her. She was
just as meticulous in her cooking. The father was again dissatisfied
and the girl was taken home. The son got angry then. He brought
home an ugly *dapom* creature the third time. When the father asked
her to cook some meat she threw it on a few cold coals and handed
it to him. "This is the wife for you," said the father. "She is not
as snooty and particular as the others. She will make you a good
wife because she will be able to stand you in any condition. She
will not make you uncomfortable with her manners."

Despite the attempts to set themselves apart from the community in assuming caste prerogatives the "good" families felt constantly impelled to demonstrate their distinctiveness in the eyes of the lowly by squandering wealth. Though generosity in the distribution of property is necessary for the maintenance of *ɔngop* rank this liberality reaches a point of "conspicuous waste"[18] in the making of favorite sons (*ɔdeitadl*) and daughters (*ɔdeimatwn*).[19] The selection of special individuals by wealthy families upon whom they lavished constant attention and for whose glorification they squandered great wealth can only be understood as a part of the battle for prestige. There were few genuine *ɔdei* in the tribe for the requirements strained all the resources of a rich family. Horses had to be given away at the child's birth. The women who came to play with the child had to be given horses. People in the camp repeatedly tested the child's reputation as *ɔdei* which the father was trying to establish, giving it trivial gifts or bestowing little attentions on the child to be showered with expensive gifts in return. Every stage in the *ɔdei*'s life no matter how inconsequential was punctuated with give-aways: the first bird the boy killed, the first time he mounted a horse, the first time he killed a buffalo, the first war party he attended, his first sex experience, when he joined a society, etc. For the girl, there were analogous occasions: the first buffalo hide she scraped, the first time she participated in a scalp dance, and so on in both cases through marriage, for the rest of their parents' lives.

In keeping with the establishment of a leisure class pattern the *ódei* was expected to do nothing, to be clothed in the most luxurious taste, to be fed delicacies most difficult to procure. The *ódei* was never punished for any misdeeds. His family kept him in a specially ornamented tipi, anticipated his every wish, and was careful not to awaken him in the morning. Hunting was too undignified and prosaic for him, and war was too dangerous. As a result, the *ɔdei* generally grew up to be helpless and quite useless, hardly capable of taking an active part in any phase of the community's life. But this, far from detracting from an *ɔngop* family's name, added to its

---

[18] The similarity between many features of Kiowa rank and the picture portrayed in VEBLEN'S *Theory of the Leisure Class* is striking.

[19] See Appendix. Three of the 25 most eminent men of the tribe were listed because of their fame as *ídeitadli*.

prominence, proving its power to withstand a great drain of wealth and to support non-productive individuals.[20]

The loss of rank in Kiowa society is quite as formally patterned as its attainment. Lying, stealing,[21] killing a fellow-tribesman, displaying moral weakness such as forgiving an unfaithful wife,[22] but especially cowardice, degrade a man's rank. An interesting example of the attitude involved is the case of Áiseioi. A Kiowa war party was attacked while all the warriors were asleep. The *toyopki*, Áiseioi, was able to pick up his bow and arrows, but in his haste he forgot his shield. Later when he had discovered its absence he decided to go back, but his comrades persuaded him that the danger was too great and agreed to frame a story explaining away the loss of the shield so that A would not be branded a coward and be debased in rank. A acquiesced, though ungraciously and was obsessed ever after with the notion that he would be exposed. Years later, while he was on another war party, unable to contain himself, he confessed his lie to his comrades predicting that he would die in the battle to be fought with the Mexican soldiers the next day. In that battle A performed some of the bravest deeds known to the tribe and was seriously wounded. He emerged from the battle blind but satisfied in the realization that the people who would learn of his secret would now forgive him. He had redeemed himself in battle and would be considered *ondeidɔ* again.

Many types of social offenses had no connection at all with reduction in rank. If an *ondeidɔ* violated the law of the policed hunt, he was punished by the society but he did not lose caste. Such flouting of the society's authority was thought of as a sporting thing. It is in the same light that committing adultery is viewed. It is expected that *ondei* will commit adultery more fre-

---

[20] This conspicuous waste was advanced to almost absurd limits when one *ondei* family tried to outdo another in the magnificence of its *ɔ́dei*. People would move into camp expecting to be feasted and given gifts by which they could decide which was the greater *ɔdei*. If one of the family's food and property was exhausted in the process it was ridiculed and scorned for its pretentions and for trying to live beyond its means.

[21] Non-deliberate stealing is excused. For example, Kódlpote, a prominent *topotoki*, who suffered from kelptomania associated with horses, was not debased and was tolerated by his amused tribesmen.

[22] If an *ɔ́ngop* pines for a wife who has deserted him, he becomes a laughing stock, is ridiculed and loses caste.

quently than others "because women seem to love them more." Sometimes an *ondei* will give up his rank voluntarily; this occurs in old age when he no longer desires to distribute wealth in validation of his rank.

The changes which have affected the scheme of Kiowa rank in recent times have been basic. When the boundaries of the Kiowa began to grow narrower and the Whites closed in, opportunities for raiding became scarce. Men had to depend more and more upon the natural increase for swelling their herds. Finally breeding became the only method for maintaining wealth. Sometime in the middle of the last century, then, wealth was divorced from war. The numbers of *ondei* were slowly diminished while the *ondeigupa*, the wealthy without war honors, became the highest goal of ambitious men. The older men who had won war honors maintained the edge and were still regarded aristocracy. But all eyes were turned toward the *ondeigupa* to observe the capable and vigorous men of the new age.

The formula for attaining rank was appropriately revised. The new prerequisites of rank were patience, industry, and skill in animal husbandry. The poor who now had to undergo a longer period of bondage before they became independent could ultimately arrive at the top of the functioning rank system. Taken into the household of their rich relatives their principal task was to manage the herding of horses. They were given good advice, how to increase their herds most quickly, how to break horses, how to change pasturage, etc., and they occasionally accompanied their relatives to capture wild horses. Periodically they were given a colt or a mule by the rich and in time even a few riding animals. Gradually a young man could accumulate a herd of his own.

At the present time the rank system is completely frozen. The rank held by Kiowa families at the end of the last century has become the fixed hereditary status of their descendants. Today, irrespective of their own attainments, men are spoken of as true *ondei*, coming from good families or as common Kiowa of *koon* descent. Skeptics of this mode of reckoning rank stress the extent of a man's property and jeer at the *ondei* who run about to council meetings and take an active part in tribal affairs but who have not an acre of land. In the conflict between these two contemporary patterns of rank it is evident that the old concept of the *ondei* family perpetuating itself has survived.

Appendix to Rank

RANK AND PRESTIGE

The 25 most famous men in the tribe

Name	Nature of Preeminence
1. Kódlpot	Best arrowmaker and butcher
2. Zéitkoyeip	Raider, singer, chief of *adltoyui*
3. Podltámtei	Warrior
4. Bɔɔdal	Great aristocrat, warrior, chief of *Tonkonga*
5. Tohɔɔte	Lover, raider, chief of *tseitánma*
6. T'éibodl	Wise counselor (*topotoki*)
7. Hɔgíikɔ	Best horse herder
8. Payíite	Most popular 10 medicine keeper (vows and settling disputes)
9. Tseitáinte	Warrior and raider
10. Gáyɔntai	Most handsome mounted warrior
11. Zéibatai	Best looking man at 60
12. Agátei	Best looking man at 70
13. Bohɔɔsen	Best looking man at 25
14. Tɔagyai	Famous as *ɔ́deitadli* (favored son)
15. Guíitetei	Famous as *ɔ́deitadli*
16. T'eineibɔɔdei	Famous as *ɔ́deitadli*
17. Togɔkáptɔ	A principal *topotoki*
18. Ɔngópte	A principal *topotoki*
19. Dɔháate	Medicine man and warrior
20. Séitãgai	Warrior, 10 medicine keeper, chief of *K'oitsɛ̃ka*
21. Séitainte	Warrior and *Teimpéiga* chief
22. Páitadli	Principal *topotoki*
23. Gúkat	Best hunter
24. Tonkɔ́nki	Best orator
25. Maiíitɛndei	Best horse racer

This list includes men living about 1870.

Topotoki: 1, 2, 3, 6, 7, 9, 17, 18, 20, 21, 22, 25, twelve in all or practically all the topotoki in the tribe. But only four were famous as topotoki— 6, 17, 18, 22.

All *ondei* except 10, 14, 15, 16, 24.

All sons of *ondei* except the following doubtful: 1, 7, 10, 20, 23, 24.

Number known for war achievements......................... 7

Non-war specialties.. 9

For good looks... 4

For political ability....................................... 4

Fame associated with horses, herding and racing.............. 2

Society chiefs.. 5

Medicine men... 3

NOTE: Kuito who acted as informant in this experiment added the name of Ɔnsokáptɔ, the *taime* keeper after it was pointed out to him that he had neglected to mention his name. K explained that the *taime* keeper is always one of the most important men of the tribe.

NOTE: Great attention paid to good looks with special standards for different ages.

Number of wives each possessed as follows:

1......2	6......2	11.....1	16.....0	21.....3
2......2	7......?	12.....1	17.....3	22.....3
3......?	8......1	13.....1	18.....3	23.....1
4......1	9......2	14.....0	19.....1	24.....1
5......1	10.....2	15.....0	20.....3	25.....2

TOTAL: 12 had one wife or none; 11 had more than one wife; 5 had more than two wives; 2 doubtful.

This aspect of the experiment is conclusive. Polygamy on the general population never rose to more than 10 per cent; 50 per cent of the "25" are polygamous.

The most famous women

1. T'ósopanti......... Tipi-making
2. Bok'íha........... Women's crafts: tanning, tipi-making, saddles
3. Ákutai........... Tanning
4. Emáatei........... Tipi-making and saddles
5. Litɔ́ .... Tipi-making and saddles
6. Somíitei........... Tipi-making and saddles
7. Eikiníitei......... Saddles
8. Máigudltei........ Saddles
9. Ɔ́ghɔtei .... Saddles
10. Mɔk'ɔ́ntei .... Bead work
11. Kótedeitei......... Bead work
12. Sɔ́biodl .... Bead work
13. Dómeidai......... Good looks

14. Ɔnkíma............   Good looks
15. Ɔkɔ́ɔtei............   Good looks
16. Tɔnk'ɔdwdltei .....   Good looks
17. Ándɔyi............   Good looks
18. Ɔ́nbodlma.........   War-whooping expert
19. Akɔ́nbai...........   Shinny player, war and scalp dancer
20. Teiyɔ́.............   Shinny player, war and scalp dancer
21. Toyái..............   Cook (bread)

TOTAL: 13 famous for proficiency in women's crafts; 5 famous for good
looks; 3 famous for women's sports.

All these women were *ondei* except 3, 5, 6, 8, 10, 16, 18.

Checking the names of their husbands proved that they were all the
wives of *ondei* except 3, 5, 6, 8, 10, 16, 18 (compare above). The asso-
ciation of the rank of the women with that of their husbands appears to
check.

VI. Rank and Warfare in the Plains: Conclusions

Before the Plains Indians entered into their period of final decline and were forcibly shut up within reservation walls in order to make way for White expansion, there was by no means an unchanging and homogeneous culture to be found among them. Nor is it to be inferred that a long period of cultural stability and historic unity in the Plains preceded the coming of the White man and the inevitable conflict that flared up. The history of the Plains is reminiscent of the development of some center of ancient civilization, a fertile valley constantly attracting one people and another by its wealth and resources. Immigrations and conquests, assimilation and reassimilation of new peoples and new traits are the signposts in its history, divergent influences causing now one pattern to stand out as dominant in one epoch, a second in another. For the Plains was essentially just such a fertile region. Its wide expanse covered with rich grasses made it the natural habitat of buffalo and provided an almost endless source of food supply. Rude horticultural techniques produced adequate results in some parts of the region. Then the coming of the horse revolutionized the life of the people.

The Plains cultures which appeared to the first White men were suffering from the effects of overnight changes. Toward the east the horticultural village peoples (Arikara, Pawnee, Osage, Omaha, etc.) were hesitantly surrendering their settled economy in favor of horse-hunting and were busily engaged in raiding the western tribes to obtain sufficient horses to take up the nomadic life. They were in turn being pressed and robbed of their grain resources by the nomads. Other tribes such as the Cheyenne and Arapaho apparently achieved the complete transformation and became full-fledged horse nomads and hunters. These latter together with other Algonkin and some Siouan peoples pushed westward elbowing aside all tribes in their way and finally meeting the Plateau Salish at the extreme border of the western Plains. A long struggle ensued; for the Salish who had just descended from the Plateau and had accumulated large horse herds offered lucrative bait. In the end they were driven back and the eastern invaders stayed, having profited well by the horse wealth of the Plateau Salish. Marginal peoples were not always treated so summarily: woodlands tribes who entered the Plains held their own. Again in the southern Plains the Kiowa and Comanche representing tribes with no horticultural tradition had found their way to the richest supply of horses partially by intent, partially by being driven south by hostile peoples. Meanwhile, a process, probably old and well-established in the Plains, of the splitting up of peoples, (the Siouan groups are especially notorious for this) and to a lesser extent the amalgamation of tribes, went on apace. The White man was contributing his share to this confused and violent epoch but other factors were present in the situation to accentuate its turbulence. The horse was one of the most important of these.

The pastoralization of Plains culture affected the whole gamut of social relations and particularly warfare and rank. It is precisely because the extent of this pastoralization has not been fully appreciated that the nature of Plains warfare and its relation to rank have been imperfectly understood. Interpretations of rank and warfare have in the main proceeded from the premise that we are dealing with simple hunting economies. Such interpretations have defined rank and warfare in the Plains without due respect to the horse.

Much of the confusion which is to be found in analyzing the nature of Plains warfare flows from blurring three distinct sets of factors. There is first the cause of war, second, a war path pattern, and finally the individual motives of the warriors. Although all three factors may overlap or even be synonymous at certain points, the distinction can often be made with meaning. As an example of such a method of analysis we may examine Osage warfare.[1] Among the Osage three types of war parties were carried on: (1) a large revenge party in the summer organized by two mourners, (2) a Sacred Bag war party which resembled (1) but was led by one mourner, was less elaborate and smaller and only a few such parties might be organized at any season and (3) expedi-

---

[1] G. A. DORSEY, *The Osage Mourning—War ceremony*, Am. Anthropologist, V. 4, 1902.   J. O. DORSEY, *An account of the War Customs of the Osages*, Am. Naturalist, V. 18, 1884. LaFLESCHE, *The Osage Tribe: Rite of Vigil*, RBAE, V. 39, 1917. SPECK, *Notes on the Ethnology of the Osage Indians*, Transactions, Univ. Pa. Museum, V. 2.

tion after horses which might occur at any time and was led by as many captains as wished to join the party, each being regarded as a mourner. The pattern of the war path is therefore in each case revenge: one mourned for property as well as persons, and vengeance had to be taken for the loss of either. To conclude that there was no economic cause for war among the Osage is obviously to fail to distinguish between cause and pattern. As for the motivations of the individual warrior, several alternatives were open to him. He might join a horse stealing expedition for the purpose of killing an enemy for only this deed would satisfy his grief in losing a favorite horse. On the other hand he might prefer to seize a good string of horses from the enemy. Again he might be specifically interested in striking coup. Or he might have no special object in mind, joining the party merely to share in the general glory and prestige that come with participation in a successful war party. The absence of unanimity in personal objectives would similarly apply to membership in a party of type (1). An individual joins an expedition to avenge the death of some important chief in hope that he may be able to claim a horse.

In the western Plains among the Cheyenne, Arapaho, Crow, etc., the horse raiding type of warfare was relatively "secularized" in the sense that it was considered in a category apart from revenge. Hence two patterns of the war path were known, each with its own procedure.[2] To continue in the vein of the Osage distinctions, duality of pattern among the western tribes need not always reflect duality of causes for war. An expedition for vengeance may be only an extension of economic conflict. For example, a Pawnee party in attempting to steal Kiowa horses is surprised and a scuffle ensues in which a Kiowa is killed. The Kiowa will then organize a revenge expedition, but such an expedition beyond the fact that it had scalps as its objective is an expression of their economic hostility.[3]

The importance of the economic motivation in warfare demonstrated by data from Kiowa is clearly present in other Plains tribes. Thus "there were many brave and successful warriors of the

---

[2] The customary procedure here was for horse raiding expeditions to start on foot to ride back when the warriors had made their raid. Revenge parties generally started on horseback. The Kiowa tribe and Comanche, however, start on horseback for both types.

[3] That is not to say that every revenge party is economically motivated.

Cheyenne. . . who on their war journeys tried to avoid coming into close contact with enemies, and had no wish to kill enemies. Such men went to war for the sole purpose of increasing their possessions by capturing horses; that is, they carried on war as a business—for profit."[4] In the autobiographical sketch of one of Kroeber's Gros Ventre informants, according to the writer's count, eighteen military expeditions were mentioned of which sixteen were raiding parties and only two revenge.[5] Wissler speaking of the Blackfoot says, ". . . the stealing of horses was almost a synonym for war. . . ."[6] Dr. Weltfish points out that the Pawnee were overwhelmingly concerned with economic aggrandizement[7] in their warfare.

The terms of peace treaties often disclose the causes for war in a direct way. The Crow-Assiniboine peace which took place about 1850, and to which the Blackfoot were apparently a party, illustrates the weightiness of the economic factors leading to war.[8] By this peace the Crow expected to receive permission to hunt in Assiniboine country unmolested by the Blackfoot. They would gain the privilege of passing through Assiniboine country to the Hidatsa in quest of corn. Finally they would have two enemies less to contend with from whom they would not have to guard their great herds of horses. The Assiniboine favored the peace because the Crow would winter with them, run buffalo with their own horses (the Assiniboine were poor in horses) and give them large quantities of meat and hides. The Crow were superior warriors and as allies would make the Assiniboine formidable against other enemies. The fact that they would be given horses every year by the Crow to preserve the peace was by no means the least gratifying advantage of the peace.

Historically viewed this position receives further support. In prehorse times the Plains could hardly have known raiding for property.[9] The type of warfare common to the marginal areas is

---

[4] GRINNELL, op. cit., V. 2, p. 2.

[5] KROEBER, Ethnology of the Gros Ventre, Bull-Robe's Narrative.

[6] WISSLER, Material Culture of the Blackfoot Indians, AP, AMNH, U. S., V. 5, p. 155.

[7] Personal communication.

[8] DENIG, op. cit.

[9] Nomadic tribes may have indulged in some sporadic stealing of the village tribes' food stores.

clearly expressed in the attitude of the Menomini who had "small interest in loot since their enemies had little or nothing better than they themselves possessed."[10] Revenge seems to have been the significant cause of warfare. There is no reason to deny the existence of some economic motivation in the warfare of early times for it was quite possible that trespassing on hunting grounds by alien peoples (which often occurred later) led to hostile contacts and killings. But with the coming of the horse a new cause for war arose which in some places functioned under the old revenge pattern (notably Osage) and in other parts of the Plains became not only a new and dominant cause but gave rise to a new pattern of warfare as well.

Stressing the economic character of warfare does not imply total rejection of the game aspect in Plains warfare. Rank goes with successful participation in war and war is principally economic. Yet to pursue the syllogism and to insist that rank is therefore purely economic in character would be empirically false. Plains warfare contains an element of the game in it. Rules of fighting and the code of conduct dictating the behavior of fighting men often has no direct relationship to the more earthy causes and motives of war.[11] The formalized deeds have a significant place in the practice of warfare and are prerequisites in the attainment of rank so far as the individual is concerned. In short, within the economic framework of war there functioned a system of warrior etiquette and formal accomplishment the successful performance of which was essential to rank. It might be suggested only incidentally that certain of the formal deeds, coup and scalping, for example, which in early times might have had crucial magical significance (men capturing others' supernatural powers by these acts) have become rather mechanical recently. The extent of the formalization of these deeds might partially be the result of the

---

[10] SKINNER AND SATTERLEE, *Folklore of the Menomini Indians*, AP, AMNH, V. 13.

[11] Sometimes the relationship is very close. For example, Lowie asks: "But why did a Crow risk his neck to cut loose a picketed horse in the midst of the hostile camp when he could easily have driven off a whole herd from the outskirts?" LOWIE, *Primitive Society*, p. 356. The answer, it appears to me, is implicit in Grinnell's statement that the most "daring" and "acquisitive" men would go into the center of an enemy's camp to cut the horses tied before the tipi. Undoubtedly this was a more daring deed but at the same time a more profitable one, because a man's best horse was tied to a stake inside the camp. See GRINNELL, V. 2, p. 15.

exaggerated economic factor in warfare and the separation of the war pattern from its older cultural context.

The relationship of the economic factor in war to the game element contains no contradiction. A parallel case is to be seen in the warfare of European feudal society in which warfare is again predominantly economic, revolving around the struggle for land, and a code of chivalry and war honors is practiced within its limits absorbing the fighting men to the apparent exclusion of all else. As in the Plains the successful practice of this code is a necessary condition for ennoblement. A contradiction could be drawn from this discussion only if the causes for war are confused with the reasons why individual men fight.

Prestige status and property control are almost universally associated. Even stratified social groupings, which are essentially noneconomic, seem generally to be linked with property factors. In the case of the Plains, rank distinctions similarly involve economic differentiation. Because war, above all, yielded property returns, the men who achieved formal military status also accumulated wealth. The adhesion of wealth to rank which no doubt previously had centered around war prowess alone changed the character and influence of rank.

Classes[12] arose with differing relationships to the economic process (master-servant, poor relative-rich relative). The attainment of high rank became a prerogative of the superior class. The wealthy class could afford to set their offspring on the path of military careers while the poor, for the most part, were compelled to specialize in the prosaic activities, hunting, camp duties, etc. The propertied group could advance the interests of their descendants because they controlled the channels of publicity. Finally, the achievement of great war reknown and the winning of leadership in war opened the way to further wealth accumulation.

---

[12] It is to be understood that I am here using a purely objective definition of class, distinguishing positions of groups with regard to the control of property and the economic process. The subjective definition of class has been made use of by MAX WEBER (Wirtschaft u. Gesellschaft, V. 3, Chap. 4) and is held in this country by MacIVER, *Society*, A Text Book, p. 166–167, and by Ralph Linton, The Study of Man, pp. 110–111, among others. This definition would simply equate class with class-consciousness. Actually, the latter only arises out of unremitting and increasingly irresoluble class conflict. The presence of both class and class-consciousness in Kiowa society (See Chapter V) merely enhances the objective reality of class and indicates roughly the measure of conflict that exists.

Thus the mechanism for rank perpetuation acted to create an aristocratic caste. Not only did this caste possess social, economic and religious characteristics of its own but it took on, at least in its own eyes, temperamental and even racial distinctiveness.

This analysis offers some specific materials for the understanding of a broad sociological topic, the emergence of class and caste differences. First, the pouring into Plains society of tangible wealth in the form of horses furnished the ground on which property distinctions could arise.[13] Next, the conjunction of property acquisition with military activity laid the basis for the ultimate creation of a wealthy hereditary elite. However, this origin suggestion has only been incidental to the main purpose of this paper. In it I have been primarily interested in following an approach which views culture in terms of interworking influences and complex relations. In Plains society, the horse, rank and warfare are inextricably interwoven and the analysis of their relations throws new light on the cultural process.

---

[13] I have tried to show in my ms. "Kiowa Economics" that acquisition of horses fit into patterns of both collective and individual initiative. Since the chief source of horses was through raiding, a phase of life in which the individual pattern predominated, the foundation for differentiation of a propertied and propertyless class was made firmer.

Works Cited

CATLIN, GEORGE. *North American Indians, being letters and notes on their manners, customs and conditions, written during eight-years travel amongst the wildest tribes of Indians in North America, 1832–39.* 2 vol., Edinburgh, 1926.

Congressional Records. Report of Commissioner of Indian Affairs, 1860–1900.

DENIG, E. T. *Indian Tribes of the Upper Missouri.* Forty-sixth Annual Report of the Bureau of American Ethnology, Washington, 1930.

DOBRIZHOFFER, MARTIN. *An Account of the Abipones, an Equestrian People of Paraguay.* 3 vol., London, 1822.

DORSEY, G. A. *The Osage Mourning-War Ceremony.* American Anthropologist, N. S., vol. 4, 1902.

DORSEY, J. O. 1. *Omaha Sociology.* Third Annual Report of the Bureau of American Ethnology, Washington, 1884.

——— 2. *An Account of the War Customs of the Osages.* American Naturalist, vol. 17, 1884.

——— 3. *Mourning and War Customs of the Kansas.* Ibid., vol. 19, 1885.

——— 4. *A Study of Siouan Cults.* Eleventh Annual Report of the Bureau of American Ethnology, Washington, 1894.

EASTMAN, M., *Dahcotah; or Life and Legends of the Sioux.* 1849.

FLETCHER, ALICE C., and LA FLESCHE, FRANCIS. *The Omaha Tribe.* Twenty-seventh Annual Report of the Bureau of American Ethnology, Washington, 1905.

GREGG, JOSIAH. *Commerce of the Prairies; or, The Journal of a Santa Fé Trader.* 2 vol., New York, 1845.

GRINNELL, GEORGE BIRD. *Cheyenne Indians, Their History and Ways of Life.* 2 vol. New Haven, 1923.

HAINES, FRANCIS. 1. *Where Did the Plains Indians Get Their Horses?* American Anthropologist, N. S., vol. 40, no. 1, 1938.

——— 2. *The Northward Spread of Horses among the Plains Indians.* Ibid., vol. 40, no. 3, 1938.

HARRINGTON, JOHN P. 1. *On Phonetic and Lexical Resemblance between Kiowa and Tanoan.* American Anthropologist, N. S., vol. 12, 1910.

——— 2. *Vocabulary of the Kiowa Language.* Bulletin 84, Bureau of American Ethnology, Washington, 1928.

HAYDEN, F. V. *Contributions to the Ethnography and Philology of the Indian Tribes of the Missouri Valley.* Philadelphia, 1863.

KROEBER, A. L. 1. *The Arapaho.* Bulletin, American Museum of Natural History, vol. 18, parts 1 and 2, New York, 1902.

——— 2. *Ethnology of the Gros Ventre.* Anthropological Papers, American Museum of Natural History, vol. 1, part 4, New York, 1908.

LA FLESCHE, FRANCIS. *The Osage Tribe: Rite of Vigil.* Thirty-ninth Annual Report of the Bureau of American Ethnology. Washington, 1925.

LEFEBRE DES NOËTTES, RICHARD. *L'attelage; le cheval de selle à travers les âges; contribution a l'histoire de l'esclavage.* Préface de Jérôme Carcopino, Paris, 1931.

LINTON, RALPH. *The Study of Man.* New York, 1936.

LOWIE, ROBERT H. 1. *The Assiniboine.* Anthropological Papers, American Museum of Natural History, vol. 4, part 1, 1909.

——— 2. *Social Life of the Crow Indians.* Ibid., vol. 9, 1912.

Lowie, Robert H. 3. *The Religion of the Crow Indians*. Ibid., vol. 15, 1922.

―――― 4. *Minor Ceremonies of the Crow Indians*. Ibid., vol. 21, 1924.

―――― 5. *Primitive Society*. New York, 1927.

―――― 6. *The Crow Indians*, New York, 1935.

MacIver, R. M. *Society, A text book of sociology*. New York, 1937.

Matthews, W. *Ethnography and Philology of the Hidatsa Indians*. U. S. Geological and geographical survey of the territories, Miscellaneous Publications, vol. 7, Washington, 1877.

Maximilian, Prince of Wied. *Travels in the Interior of North America*. Translated from the German by H. E. Lloyd, London, 1843. [Edited by Reuben Gold Thwaites, 3 vol., Cleveland, 1905. (Early Western Travels, vol. 22, 23, 24)]

McLeod, W. C. *The American Indian frontier*. New York, 1928.

Mézières y Chuguy, Athanase de. *Athanase de Mézières and the Louisiana-Texas Frontier, 1768–1780*, in Spain in the West, a Series of Original Documents from Foreign Archives, vol. 1–2, Cleveland, 1914–1929. Herbert Eugene Bolton, translator and editor.

Mooney, James. *Calendar History of the Kiowa Indians*. Seventeenth Annual Report of the Bureau of American Ethnology, part 1, Washington, 1898.

Radin, Paul. *The Winnebago Tribe*. Thirty-seventh Annual Report of the Bureau of American Ethnology, 1923.

Ray, Verne F. *The Sanpoil and Nespelem: Salishan Peoples of Northeastern Washington*. University of Washington Publications in Anthropology, vol. 5, Seattle, 1932.

Le Raye, Charles. *Journal of Charles Le Raye*. South Dakota Historical Collection, vol. 55, 1908.

Richardson, R. N. *The Comanche Barrier to South Plains Settlement*. 1933. Glendale, Calif.

Riggs, S. R. *Dakota Grammar, texts and ethnography*. Contributions to North American ethnology, vol. 9, Washington, 1893.

Skinner, Alanson, and Satterlee, John V. *Folklore of the Menomini Indians*. Anthropological Papers, American Museum of Natural History, vol. 13, 1915.

Smith, Marian W. *The War Complex of the Plains Indians*. Proceedings, American Philosophical Society, vol. 78, 1938.

Speck, Frank G. *Notes on the Ethnology of the Osage Indians*. Transactions, Department of Archeology, University of Pennsylvania, vol. 2, part 2, 1907.

Strong, W. D. *An Introduction to Nebraska Archeology*. Smithsonian Miscellaneous Collections, vol. 93, no. 10, Washington, 1935.

Teit, James. *The Salishan Tribes of the Western Plateaus*. Forty-fifth Annual Report of the Bureau of American Ethnology, 1930. (Franz Boas, editor)

Veblen, Thorsten. *Theory of the Leisure Class*. New York, 1899.

Weber, Max. *Wirtschaft und Gesellschaft*. Grundriss der Sozialoekonomik, vol. 3, part 1–2, Tübingen, 1925.

Weltfish, Gene. *Field notes on Pawnee Economics*.

Wissler, Clark. 1. *Material Culture of the Blackfoot Indians*. Anthropological Papers, American Museum of Natural History, vol. 5, part 1, New York, 1910.

―――― 2. *The Influence of the Horse in the Development of Plains Culture*. American Anthropologist, N. S., vol. 16, 1914.

―――― 3. *North American Indians of the Plains*. Handbook Series, no. 1. American Museum of Natural History, New York, 1922.